Good Grief

Inviting Grief to Be a Catalyst for Growth

Krista M. Powers

VITALITY
buzz, bliss + books

Good Grief: Inviting Grief to Be a Catalyst for Growth
Copyright © 2025 by Krista M. Powers
Published by VITALITY buzz, bliss + books LLC
vitalitybuzz.org

VITALITY buzz, bliss + books LLC publishes original creations to grow the mission of VITALITY Cincinnati Inc, a 501(c)3 education-based nonprofit: sharing holistic self-care from neighborhood to neighborhood, person to person, and breath by breath since 2010.

Every effort has been made to give credit to other people's original ideas through the text itself. If you feel something should be credited to someone and is not, please get in touch through our website and every effort will be made to correct this text for future printings. Thank you!

We invite you to honor your mind, your body, your whole self. Do only what you know to be right for you. While the invitations offered here in this book, on our websites and social media, and in our classes are geared to be gentle and easily modified by the participant to fit the participants' needs, please consult your medical doctor or health professional before undertaking any practices.

We are grateful to Julie Lucas of withinwonder.com who designed the cover, interior artwork, and VITALITY's logos; Dianne Powers who edited the book so beautifully, and Kyle Null who designed Krista's logo.

ISBN: 978-1-954688-40-7

CONTENTS

Intention & Request

Fairly early in life, I learned to give attention to the question: *What am I trying to accomplish?* Another version of this question: *What impact do I want to make?*

When I ventured into entrepreneurship and coaching, these core questions became integral in every space of life. Certainly, they were imperative with clients, yet I also began practicing greater intentionality with my own body, mind, spirit, relationships, money, time, energy....and on and on. As I identified what impact I was seeking to create, I noticed my ability to accomplish specific goals increased. This held true with my clients as well.

As we set forth together into *Good Grief: Inviting Grief to be a Catalyst for Growth,* I have an intention, a dream, and a request that I want to share from the onset.

My intention is to evolve our understanding and language to reflect the role grief plays in our lives.

My dream is to fundamentally shift how we engage with grief, to support growth.

If I am completely honest, I have additional hopes and dreams woven within these pages. This hope is inviting curiosity, sparking conversations, cultivating new paradigms, shifting cultural norms, and healing our world. These were the intentions of my first book, *Midlife Calm: An Alternative to Midlife Crisis.* They feel applicable here as well. Part of me giggles with what may seem to be such lofty goals. A bigger part of me stands with my feet firmly planted, shoulders back and heart open to these intentions being lived into reality. I deeply believe that we can shift our norms around grief. I hope this book adds to that revolution.

Finally, and perhaps most importantly, my request is that you trust. Trust that I am holding your grieving heart with tenderness. Trust that something from these pages will shine light on the darkness you have felt or are feeling. Trust that you are where you need to be, and this is not where you will be forever.

Dedication

To Mom & Dad

*Your ability to hold space for grief to be woven into the fabric of everyday life in a way that is whole and holy inspires me. I am eternally grateful to learn with and from you. You have modeled how to trust and love the process, which allows me to celebrate the heavy **and** the powerful moments of life.*

To the Giving Voice community

Thank you for modeling that the full expanse of emotions is possible amid a diagnosis of Alzheimer's disease, or other forms of dementia. You model what it looks like to engage with grief in new and nuanced ways, every day. You also show how powerful the human spirit is, especially when we create community and connection.

Asking for and receiving support has been one of the most beautiful and radical acts of self-love I have ever practiced. With intentionality, I have become more fluent in both, and I see how ready and willing so many are to show up for me....and for one another. In this book, you are deemed a VATRON. In my life you are called family and friend. In my heart you are the example of generosity, the joy of lived interconnectedness, and the inspiration to be a *"Yes!"* for others. Thank you for bringing this book to fruition and for being with me on this journey. My love is flowing to you!

James Aglione; Nic & Jennifer Alessandrini; Cynthia Allen & Larry Wells; Warner, Jen, & Sterling Allen; Laberta Arnold; Jackson & Skylar Athey; Jean Badik; Grace Badik; Jennifer Baltzersen; Diana Barhorst; Taylor Barker; Patrice, Jim, & Nathan Barker; Deana Barone; Megan Basmajian; Alicia Bauer; Jim & Lisa Bayne; Teri Beasley; Stephanie Beck; Denise Benavides; Amy Benetti; Lori Beran; Jenni Blake; Lisa Boh; Lindsey Bonadonna; Liz Bonis; Diana & Steve Bosse; Ellen Bourgeois; Sonya & Gregory Bracho; Megan Bradford; Shannon Braun; Deborah Breda; Holly Brians Ragusa; Logan & Matt Brown; Meghan Brown; Raegan Brown; Marge Brown; Steve Browne; Richard Brumfield; Trisha Brundage; Lynn Burkhardt; Linda Castaneda; Amy & Kerry Patrick Clark; Karl Coiscou; Jan Cook; Melba Cooke; Kristin Cooley; Holly Cousino; Sarah Creighton; Jessie Cybrowski; Richard Danford; Jennifer Danner; Annette DeCamp; Monica Denniston; Rachel DesRochers; Sue & Mark Dickey; Catie Doebler; Jesse Dunbar; Paula & Mark Dunson; Sylvia Dwertman; Denise & Mike Eck; Allison Edwards; Emily Elma; Marissa Esterline; Ursula & Ken Esterline; Jean Ann & Keith Fairchild; Erica & Tyler Fairchild; Deborah Farris; Amy & John Fecker; Nan Fischer & Rose Monnin; Mark Fisher; Loretta & Stan Flerlage; Patrick, Michael, & Coen Flerlage; Jenny Foertsch, In Loving Memory of Dick Fouse, Lacey Fox; Julie & Mark Friebel; David Furry; Stephen Gastright; Christian & Cody Gausvik; Catherine Gausvik; Cindy Geer; Anne Gerber; Terre & Emil Giglio; Kris Girrell; Anna Goubeaux; Jennifer Grafitti; Kristi Guilfoyle; Layne & Jeff Haas; Janie Hall; Heather Hallman; Dawn Hallmark; Barb Hancock; Elise Sebastian & Hanna Windhorn; Tim Hanner; Candice Hayes-McInnis; Tom & Carolyn Hayward; Julie Hermann; Christopher Hernandez; Richard Hernandez; Lisa & Abel Hernandez; Lauren & Pat Hill; Rachel Hodesh; Angela Homoelle; Julie Hopkins; Aleah Hordges;

Forrest Horn; Sandy Hostler; Elizabeth & Zac Huffman; Amy Huffman McIntosh; Natalie Jackson; Jamie Jackson; Carri Jagger; Lisa Jennings; Julie Johnson; Dana Johnson; Rhonda Johnson; Adam Johnston; Holly Jones; Arielle Jordan; Rachel Justison; Alysia Kaiser & Melisia Holt; Troy & Erin Kehr; Pam Kent; Margie Klepper; Lynn Knudsen; Kim Koenig; Laura Kroeger; Angela Lapasnick; Charmain Lee; Donna & Jim Leer; Maria Lees-Dunlap; Myke Lewis; Sandra Lingo; Tara Litmer; Julie Lucas; Chris Ludwig; Nancy Macke; Andrea Maksuymczak; Elizabeth Maksuymczak; Barb Markey; Mike & Amy Mason; Karen Mathena; Jennifer Mattingly; Beth McFarland; Stephen McIntosh; Adam "pahdnah" McNally; Julie Metzger; Jean Meyer; Katie & Bonnie Meyer; Teddy & Cindy Michel; Danny Miles; Mike Miller; Tammy Miller-Ploetz; Michele Mischler; Megan Mitchell & Izzy Wilson; Beth Montpas; Tricia Morris; Mike Napier; Jeanne Neumeyer; Peter & Kim Newberry; In Loving Memory of John Neyer; Katy Nickerson; Lisa & Randy Nocks; Candice Nonas; Sherry Northgard; Bonnie Olson; Mary Beth Ong; Dave & Kathy Palmer; Ilona Pamplona; Jon Parker; James Partin; Lea Peacock; Deborah Pearce; IVC Northeastern Pennsylvania; Jake Penwell; Danny Perkins; Emily Perl Kingsley; Elizabeth Peters; Claire Pfister; Jordan, Chris, Dalton, Ella, & Beckham Pfouts; April Plummer; Jan Powers; Kyle Powers & Josh Mallory; Thom & Dianne Powers; Gerry Preece; Iena Putkonen; Sandy Rabe; Kate Race; Martha Ragan; Melissa Ramos; Ryan Reed; Bobby Reynolds; Sunshine Richards; Sarah Rieger; Sarah Riehle; Amy Robinson; Elizabeth & John Robson; Deb Rowland; Kristin Ruminer; Heather Rutz; Dana Ruwe; Jenny Sanchez; Nune Sargsyan; Ruth Sawyer; Barbara Schroeder; Brenda Schroeder; Don Schroeder; Sr. Paulette Schroeder; Judy & Jere Schuler; Lori & Glen Schulte; Brett Sears; Cynthia Sellers; Linda Shaw; Teresa Shiffert; Brian Shircliff; Sue & Ron Shroder; Lori Shutrump; Shannon Silk; AnnMarie Simon; Lindsey & JD Simons; Marlene Sims; Kelly Sinclair; Candace, Andrew, & Ivar Sjogren; Olivia Smith; Sara Smith; In Loving Memory of Sonny, Geralyn & Tom Sparough; Evan Spaulding; Missy Spears; Jeffrey Stec; Veronica Sterling; Amy Stone; Sandi Stonebraker; Saira Sufi; Elaine Sugimura; Katherine Sweeney Grimm; Ryan Taylor; Mathew Taylor; Candice Terrell; Lori Terry; Max Traina; Evan Turell; Amanda Valentine; Susan & Derek Van Amerongen; Steve Vesschmont; Dean Violetta; Jeff Walton; Paddy Ward; Annie Warner; Demetrie Weaver; Paul Wesselmann; Laura Weyler; Jenn White-Brogan; Heather Whitlock; Breanna Williams; Tamara Williams; John & Linda Wink; Christopher Woods; Rob Workley; Jamie & Bryan Zarosley; Nan Zupancic

Introduction

"What's the opposite of up?"

This was a funny little question my dad asked me in the middle of a conversation we were having a couple years ago. Given the relationship I have with my dad, I knew this could either go down a path of an eye-rolling joke or something mind-blowingly impactful. The rest of the conversation unfolded like this:

With a slight pause, gauging where this may go, I answered, *"Down."*

He proceeded, *"What's the opposite of light?"*

I quickly responded, *"Dark."*

Dad asked, *"What's the opposite of in?"*

"Out," I said. By now I was feeling curious about how many questions would make up this litany my dad was sharing.

"What's the opposite of high?"

The back and forth had a steady pace by now. I responded, *"Low."*

Dad volleyed, *"What's the opposite of love?"*

This one made me take a beat. I confess, I have this old default mechanism within me that likes to be right. At the time of this conversation, I still *really* liked to have things figured out and even be one step ahead whenever possible. I came back with, *"Well, the first thing that comes to mind is hate or fear, but I don't think that is going to be the answer. What is it?"*

Dad looked me in the eye and said, "*Grief.*"

"*The opposite, or absence of love, is grief.*"

He went through each of the other dualities we had just breezed through to help illuminate the conversation:

The absence of up is down.
The absence of light is dark.
The absence of in is out.
The absence of high is low.
The absence of love is grief.

I was fully in. The notion stretched my mind yet...didn't. It made sense, which allowed my brain to be at ease and let it sink into my heart. Yeah, it was totally on point. This made so much heart sense. I thought of a few loved ones who had died – my grandparents, a dear friend Katie, some pets. When they were gone and it felt different to flow my love into them, I certainly did not feel fear or hate...I felt grief.

Another interesting twist comes from author and clinical psychologist, Dr. Janina Scarlet, who said, "*The opposite of love is not grief. It's disconnection. Grief is love's extension. When your heart breaks, it's because you really loved. And it also takes love to put it back together.*" (posted on Facebook: March 13, 2021)

Either way you slice it, the topic of love bubbles to the surface in the conversation of grief. So, let's meander down the path of love for a moment. I would like to offer some references regarding the complexity of love as a juxtaposition to our understanding of grief.

Love exists in many forms. In our Western culture, we cram a lot of meaning into one word. This pigeonholes us and convolutes the depth and understanding we have of love. Love can be characterized in many ways. Kristina Hallett, Ph.D., a clinical psychologist, offers two overarching categories: passionate and compassionate love. (cited by Sarah Regan in her mindbodygreen article "The 8 Types Of Love + How To Know Which One You're Feeling") Dr. Gary Chapman authored the popular book, *The 5 Love Languages*. His work supported a greater depth and understanding that people give and receive love in different ways. And perhaps the richest, most ornate relationship with love comes from the ancient Greeks who had eight categories and different words for each:

Eros: Romantic love, passion, and desire

Philia: Affectionate love, such as that between friends or family

Ludus: Playful love, such as the feeling you get when you have a crush on someone

Agape: Unconditional love for everyone, such as empathy, forgiveness, and acceptance

Pragma: Enduring love, such as a mature and lasting love between partners

Mania: Obsessive love, which can become unhealthy

Storge: Familiar love, such as the bond between family members

Philautia: Self-love

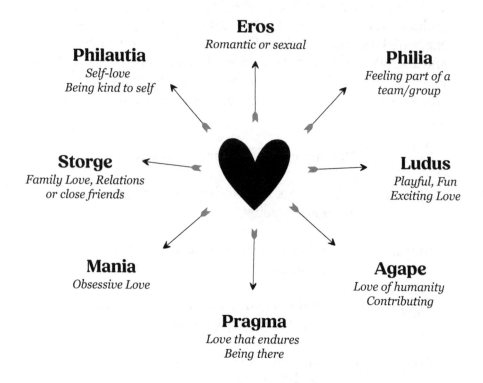

Eros
Romantic or sexual

Philautia
Self-love
Being kind to self

Philia
Feeling part of a
team/group

Storge
Family Love, Relations
or close friends

Ludus
Playful, Fun
Exciting Love

Mania
Obsessive Love

Agape
Love of humanity
Contributing

Pragma
Love that endures
Being there

Diagram inspired by Joanne Reed's
"8 Types of Love – Which One Are You?" (12/12/2020)

It's that last one that always gets me – Philautia: Self-love. I am fortunate to have grown up in a household brimming with Agape, Philia, and Storge love. Without necessarily using the Greek vernacular, I was taught about many forms of love, including Philautia. Yet, as I look around, so many of us are not acquainted or comfortable with self-love, let alone many of the other types of love the Greeks described. I wonder, what would be possible if we had a deeper understanding of love?

Like love, our culture has boiled grief down into one word with so much bundled within it. When we take a moment to look at the etymology of the word grief, we find our Middle English version comes from Old French "*grever*" which means "*to burden*". In Latin, the word grief comes from "*gravare*" which means "*to make heavy*". Our evolution of the word grief has arrived at the definition provided by Oxford Language as "*deep sorrow, especially that caused by someone's death.*" And the informal use of the word grief in our vernacular is defined as "*troubled or annoyance.*"

Yet, I am fortunate to have a dear friend who is a self-proclaimed word nerd. She suggested I go a bit deeper into the spirit of the word grief. When we pull apart the definition "*to burden*" two pathways appear – one which talks about "carrying" as it pertains to something heavy, and one which talks about bearing children, or the "*burden*" of birthing.

Whoa! Much like my dad's litany of questions had caught my attention, so too did my friend's unpacking of the word grief. It caused me to really think about the process of birth and how complex, complicated, painful, shattering, and beautiful it is. I felt a tinge of both excitement and concern as I listened to her long-refined ability to understand and share the depth of words. My concern sourced from whether others would be able to hear and accept a wider lens of grief. Heaviness *and* birthing?! My excitement flowed from what has always been within me, yet without the previous language to share it.

Jamee Mae Kyson said, "*To love someone is to attend a thousand births of who they are becoming.*"

My belief is that when we get to the root, grief is far more nuanced than we've allowed it to be. Like love, grief is not unilaterally defined. It has the essence of heaviness *as well as birth*. When a woman births a child, she undergoes physical and hormonal changes to bring something new into the world. And, she has a space left within her where that baby previously resided for nine months. There is a letting go of what was: the time and experience of gestation; and a welcoming of the new phase: a child separate from the woman who birthed the child.

In a similar way, grief is the process of letting go of one thing to make space for another. It is carrying the heaviness of loss as well as birthing new, often unknown opportunities ahead. When we begin to play with this perspective, greater possibilities arise for our relationship with grief. We become aware of the role it plays in our everyday life, and we begin to embrace versus resist it.

Grief, like birth, is part of the cycle of life. It is a yin and yang relationship of that which is complementary, contrasting, and interconnected. Without love, we would not experience grief... and vice versa. Grief is, simply put, a transition to something different or new. It occurs when you lose your loved one, get a divorce, or are laid off from a job. Grief also surfaces when you graduate from college, leave behind the single life to become a couple, or retire. These are all experiences of ending one thing and stepping forward into something new.

If I am being really radical, I'd also say grief arrives when we spill the milk, adopt the pet, say goodbye, cut our hair, or drop the kids off at school. Grief is letting go of one thing to create room for something else. Like love, it is woven into all the moments of our lives – the meaningful and miniscule.

To be clear, I am not making light of grief's impact when I say it is woven into our everyday lives or when I share examples of small happenings that interrupt our flow. Rather, I am casting light for us to more readily recognize grief, to become more familiar with it, and to release our resistance to it.

For more than a quarter century, I have said I wanted to be part of a revolution that shifts our cultural norms of aging, death, and dying. Little did I know the focus would turn out to be about grief. Which brings us to this book.

My goal is to be gentle, direct, and loving. I acknowledge that grief and loss can be triggering for some. I also acknowledge it is inescapable, which is why I seek to evolve our perspectives that allow us to embrace instead of resist when the moments of grief arise in our lives.

If you have cried your heart out during a transition – this book is for you. If you have wondered what it would be like to make a radical departure from a path you are on – this book is for you. If you have agonized over an upcoming change – this book is for you. And, if you have buried someone you love – this book is for you. *Good Grief: Inviting Grief to Be a Catalyst for Growth* is for all humans, not just those confronting death. It is for those seeking solace as well as those who have not yet encountered the pangs that accompany loss.

You see, this book is not singularly about death, yet the topic is thread throughout the pages. Literal death and figurative death are a cornerstone of the experience of transition and grief. So, it is necessary to dive into this topic.

Some of the stories within this book may bring forward your own memories. My invitation is to allow them to flow. If tears are present or you need a break, set the book down and give yourself the space you need. Just know, when you return, the words written here are meant to gently tend to whatever feels raw within you. The intention is to evolve our language, understanding, and experience of grief. My dream is to fundamentally shift how we engage with grief, to support growth.

In this book I will share some of the work that has been done in the realm of grieving and extend a new perspective on this part of what it means to be human. I will share stories and examples, with a goal of viewing grief from a different perspective and inviting a new way of looking at your own grief. And I will offer The 5 Powers of Grief. I do not believe I have it all figured out. I welcome the evolution and co-creation of these Powers of Grief. These simply come from a few decades of serving in the

Field of Aging and Dying, as well as my own lived experiences of grief in the form of thyroid and breast cancer, divorce, and many other moments of grief and loss. I've been curious through each moment to glean the greater lessons of grief and from that I offer The 5 Powers of Grief:

1. **The Interruption**

2. **Flow of Feelings**

3. **Holding**

4. **Breaking**

5. **Re-Membering**

Before going any further, I should acknowledge that I have officially created a pattern. It seems I like to create witty or thought-provoking book titles and then immediately debunk them! When I wrote *Midlife Calm: An Alternative to Midlife Crisis*, I knew the message was about creating calm in any age and stage of life, yet I was also committed to introducing the term Midlife Calm and would not abandon the title. While writing this book, I have been very aware there is no such thing as "good" or "bad" grief. There's just grief. It was also brought to my attention that, for some, the title conjures up Charlie Brown's utterance every time Lucy pulled the football out from under his swinging leg or something unfortunate happened in his comic strip life. Indeed, Charlie Brown was cast with a pessimistic outlook, quickly sharing frustration and annoyance in everyday life. His frequent display of dismay or disbelief so readily expressed through his signature phrase, "*Good grief!*" may resonate with some. For others, this reference does not land. Either way, please feel free to join me in dismissing the title and diving into the real meat of the message. I am genuinely grateful we are on this journey together.

The simple, yet profound perspective my dad offered me about love and grief was a paradigm shift...which is what I intend to offer within the pages of this book. Through new ideas, stories, and questions I will always return to the intention of evolving our understanding and language to reflect the role grief plays in our lives. My dream is very alive.

With this intention as our beacon, I again ask you trust that I am holding your grieving heart with tenderness. Trust that something from these pages will shine light on the darkness you have or are feeling. Trust that you are where you need to be now, though it is not where you will be forever. May this book honor all the nuances and beauty of our humanity.

Thank you for your trust.

1

Grief:
A Companion on Our Journey

I had a sense that the call was not going to be good news. It was 6:20 on a Monday evening, a time when most doctors' offices are closed, and specialists were ideally at home after a day of tending to their strenuous jobs.

I had spent the past 10 days juggling unexpected appointments while also putting the final touches on a weekend retreat I was co-hosting for a group of 10 women. The retreat was the second annual, titled CONNECT 2.0. I planned to meet my two co-facilitators, and dear friends, on Thursday to ground ourselves for the weekend ahead. We would arrive at the venue, three hours from my home in Northern Kentucky, Friday morning and ensure the space was prepared for our guests to arrive on Friday afternoon and settle in for 48 hours of connecting. Our goals were to facilitate an environment for women to connect with themselves by releasing, surrendering, and opening up space for all that life holds, and to dive into the science and embodiment of holistic care and renewal. We had spent a year planning for this weekend of play, nature, rest, and connection.

Yet, I was coming in a mess! Who knows how, but I had a brush with poison ivy that had invaded my hands, arms, torso, thighs, neck, and face. For nearly two weeks, I deployed every known remedy to soothe what was an ever-expanding rash. I was on my second steroid pack, each 10-day regimen aimed at kicking the problem, only to cause a different dilemma of insomnia. I was desperate though, and willing to do anything to get rid of the poison ivy. It was not a pretty situation.

Although the poison ivy was a massive inconvenience, it was something I had experienced before and felt the only option was to forge ahead and show up for the women who had invested their time and money in the retreat weekend. Perhaps the ironic twist of this story is that my portion of the retreat was to facilitate the part about release, surrender, and opening up space – all of which was rooted in the topic of grief.

You see, the Saturday prior to the retreat, I felt a lump in my right breast. It was a surreal moment since I wasn't actually doing a self-breast exam, rather was just randomly feeling my own body. I felt it once, and then again. I told myself not to panic, as I interrupted whatever light-hearted thing my partner Patrick and I were talking about. Without revealing what I had discovered, I asked him to feel my breast. Sensing this was not a romantic gesture, he obliged and in his regular calm demeanor confirmed that there was something there. I committed out loud, *"I'll call my doctor first thing Monday morning. I don't think Urgent Care could do anything."*

Falling asleep that night was hard. My mind raced. I attempted every mindfulness and breathing exercise I knew. Eventually I slept, only to have the lump as the first thing on my mind upon waking Sunday. A quick feel confirmed it was still there, and rather large in my opinion. I sent a message to my doctor on MyChart so she would see it first thing Monday, and then did my best to preoccupy myself the rest of the day.

Thankfully, someone from my doctor's office called early Monday morning. With their help, I got in for a mammogram on Tuesday. It took much longer than my annual mammograms, as the technician diligently took her time and had me keep my smock on while I waited for the results to be read. Sitting in that waiting room, my mind bolted from thought to thought.

Was it cancer?
Should someone be here with me?
Don't jump to conclusions.

Calm down.
Breathe.
Do I want to call Patrick? Or mom and dad? Or my sister?
Or Aunt Ursula – she's been through this.

I was called back for a second mammogram and an ultrasound, which I knew was the easiest procedure I'd have done – just lay there and have gel placed on the reader that rolled over my skin. With one arm raised, the technician offered assuring words as she added pressure to get accurate pictures. She stepped out at one point and returned to get a few more images. With gentleness in her voice, she guided me to go ahead and get dressed and brought me to a private office with a table in one corner and two comfortable chairs in the other. She said a doctor would be with me shortly.

I didn't like the progression of this appointment. I was there for a mammogram to check a lump I found. Yet here I was 45 minutes later waiting for a doctor to come talk to me after a second mammogram and additional test? It didn't feel good. Plus, I had a retreat to prepare for and other work projects that needed my attention. Oh yeah, I also had a nasty poison ivy rash all over me!

The medical resident came in and sat with me. She talked slowly. She said that the mammogram and ultrasound were inconclusive, and they needed to refer me for a biopsy. I looked at the paper in front of me that required my signature to proceed with the next referral. I felt torn between relief and doom. Inconclusive – that was good! There was nothing yet to be truly worried about. A needle in my breast – that was not good! I hated needles and I was officially overwhelmed. The tears welled up and poured down my cheeks. She handed me a tissue and told me we could take as much time as I needed. I didn't even know what to ask, though I floundered through a few things like, *"Will you explain to me again what the mammogram and ultrasound readings said?"* and *"When will I have the biopsy?"* Finally, *"Will it hurt?"* I don't get unnerved easily, but at this moment – after 60 hours of attempting to hold it together - I could feel myself quickly unraveling.

Two days later, I drove myself in for the biopsy. I warned the assistant that I was covered in poison ivy and asked if that would be a problem? She assured me that it would not be, though she offered her sympathy for how angry my skin was. She talked me through exactly what was going to happen and said she would be in the room the whole time. I told her how nervous I was and asked if she would hold my hand during the biopsy. When the doctor came in, he was kind and patient. He reiterated each step and asked if I had any questions. He said he would walk me through everything he was doing as it happened. When we were done, they shared that results often take 48 hours. Since it was midday Thursday, they could not promise I would have an answer before the weekend, but I would get a call for sure by Monday.

That weekend, with red poison ivy rash radiating skin, I facilitated a retreat about grief. It was the first group to ever hear and engage with The 5 Powers of Grief. It wasn't perfect, though it was impactful. I held myself together in the midst of so many emotions flowing through me as I anxiously awaited biopsy results that indeed did not come through before the start of the weekend. Looking back, the foreshadowing was thick. The lump in my breast was a massive interruption – one that was about to catapult me into The 5 Powers of Grief, like it or not.

When Monday came, I kept my phone in hand all day. As the hours passed, my insides churned with anxiety, frustration, anticipation, and an ever present, though dwindling, sliver of hope that this would all be ok. Around 4pm, I received a message in MyChart. The doctor who conducted the biopsy the previous Thursday had assured me that I would get a call, no matter the outcome. He encouraged me to try to refrain from deciphering the results myself if they were populated in MyChart before I received a phone call. Yet, as 5pm approached, and no call yet received, I took it upon myself and opened the report in MyChart. As I sifted through the medical jargon - first describing that the doctor had reviewed all potential complications with me, next outlining the steps conducted in the procedure - I finally arrived at words that seemed to say the tumor was malignant.

I felt hollow. I sat in silence the next 30 minutes until Patrick arrived home from work. I told him what I had read. He attempted to ground me by saying we needed to talk to a doctor before mentally racing down any path. I'm not sure I needed to be grounded though. I was still and quiet, although a bit unclear as to what to do next. Nothing felt important anymore. Except, I was so angry that Monday had come and gone and I did not get a call.

Until I did.

At 6:20pm, to my surprise, a number from my provider popped up on my phone. I sat at the dining room table and answered. It was the doctor who had done the biopsy the week before. He apologized for calling so late and asked if I had read anything in MyChart. I thanked him for calling after hours and admitted I had looked. He confirmed what I had read on my own and apologized for having to share this news. He then said I would be getting a call from an oncologist to make a plan.

It was a short call, with Patrick looking on from the kitchen. When I hung up, it took a few moments but then...I sobbed.

This book is not going to be all about me and my journey of healing with and through breast cancer – though I will share a bit more of that story within these pages. No, this is about our relationship with grief – literal and figurative deaths. It's about the many monumental and minuscule moments within our days where grief is present. By now you know it has been a topic that's long been on my mind and heart. Heck, I already had a well enough developed outline of The 5 Powers of Grief to lead a retreat in July 2023!

With the goal of setting the stage for our conversation about grief, I will share a few additional stories.

When I was a Junior in college, I got the call to come home soon if I wanted to see her one last time. She was dying. Without hesitation, I made the three-and-a-half-hour trek home the following weekend.

She was our cat of 20 years: Baby Doll. Her eyes were pristine blue and her fur was white with patches of orange on her back, tail, and face. Through the years, we watched Baby Doll birth litters of kittens, hunt in the fields, and enjoyed countless moments of cuddling and loving in the backyard. She outlived some of her own offspring and held a special role of unconditional acceptance and love in our family.

Upon arriving home, Baby Doll was curled up next to a heat vent in the bathroom. I had never seen her in the house before, largely due to the fact that my dad was highly allergic, yet also because mom grew up on a farm so pets in the house were not her vibe. Despite the promise of itchy eyes and excessive sneezing, dad loved this cat dearly. As she grew frail, it was a no-brainer to bring her into the house to wash her fur that she no longer had the energy to clean and keep her comfortable with canned, wet food.

I hold this as a core memory – arriving home, hugging mom and dad, and moving immediately to the bathroom to see Baby Doll. I sat on the floor and gently scooped her into my arms. For the next several hours I pet her, talked to her, and infused every bit of Pragma and Agape love possible into her.

It was hard leaving at the end of the weekend, knowing these would be the last moments I would spend with our beloved pet. Later that week, mom and dad called to tell me that Baby Doll had died peacefully there in the bathroom.

It wasn't until years later, as we reminisced about Baby Doll, that I became aware of an entirely different perspective around her death. Although her death was a shared experience for my nuclear family of four, it impacted each of us very differently. While I was grieving the loss of our furry-family member who had been there during every chapter of my life, my dad found himself deeply grieving. He shared that when Baby Doll died, he wept like never before. His grief was compounded with self-imposed shame for not grieving in the same, seemingly deep way when his own father and then mother died. Yet, this cat had offered my dad more unconditional love and genuine connection than his parents ever had. This is not to say they were bad people, rather they came with their own set of baggage, understanding of relationships, and abilities (or inabilities) to be present to their family in ways that fostered safe and authentic relationships.

I was rocked when dad told me how deeply Baby Doll's death impacted him. Indeed, despite the shared experience of sitting on the bathroom floor to cradle her in those final days, our experience of grief was radically different. This compelled me to inquire about the impact of Baby Doll's death on my mom and older sister, Patrice.

Mom's memory is faint and centered around the desire to be there for her spouse, who was so grief stricken. In addition to that though, Baby Doll's death summoned a moment from decades earlier in my mom's life. When she was four or five, her first and favorite pet, Buster, died. Mom remembers tucking away in a corner of the living room, crying. When her dad came in from working on the farm, he saw his little one and in his own way attempted to console her. He told her not to cry about it...it was just an animal. He was not unkind, rather, likely unsure how to deal with the loss of his beloved companion as well as his child's suffering. All of this is what came rushing back for my mom in the midst of caring deeply for my dad and saying goodbye to such an important part of our family.

My sister had moved out of our family home at the time, so

Baby Doll was no longer part of her everyday life. Of course, she visited and remembers Baby Doll's sweet disposition and beautiful blue eyes, both of which were frail and a bit more muted in her final weeks and days. Patrice reflects, "*She seemed smaller and frail...her voice was smaller too.*" Yet, we both knew how lucky we were to have had so many years with her.

Patrice went on to share that it wasn't so much grief she felt as it was a reflection on Baby Doll's life and role in our family, and how her final days played out. From my sister's perspective, our cats were always outdoor pets because dad was so allergic. We all had to be careful to wash our hands after petting the cats, so Dad's eyes and nose would not get irritated with the faintest bit of dander. As Baby Doll came to the end of her life, with Mom and Dad tenderly caring for her, Patrice remembers how poignant it was for dad to set aside his own comfort for our kitty's care.

When Baby Doll died, Dad buried her in the backyard under a tree close to the house. That was in 1998. It wasn't until writing this book in 2025 that we heard each other's perspectives and experiences of this shared grief. I feel beautifully cracked open hearing my mom, dad, and Patrice talk about their memories of those final days...and the deeper story of what caused and allowed them to grieve her death.

There's so much to say about the experience of death. Yet also in moments, there are no words to be spoken. Death leaves a void in the shape of the person or dream we held close. It creates a flood of emotions, both immediate and overtime. Death has the power to freeze us in time and thrust us into the future. It reveals a new way, whether we like it or not.

Baby Doll was not the first death experience I had encountered. In fact, in talking to others through the years, I realized I was well acquainted with death early on. Not because I was surrounded by an exorbitant amount, but rather because my parents chose to expose my sister and me to every aspect of life. We were taught that death is a part of life, so we attended funerals alongside Mom and Dad when a family or friend transitioned.

My mom and dad tell the story of when I was probably three years old and three feet tall. My sister and I quietly entertained ourselves while my parents circulated the crowd at a funeral home visitation. When the time came for us to approach the casket and pay our respects to the distant relative who had lived a long life, I found the velvety fabric that folded out from the casket liner. Being drawn to soft tactiles and the perfect height, I rubbed my face against the fabric as I waited for mom and dad to have their moment of silence looking onto the body resting in the casket. What can I say? I like soft things! It did not phase me that someone we knew and loved was just inches away, no longer of this earth.

When I did a year of volunteer service after college, I worked for an organization that served people with HIV and AIDS. Melba Cooke, my supervisor who was affectionately known as Cooke, was a direct and kind human. Her hearty laugh and big hugs made everyone feel seen and loved. I remember attending my first funeral for a client. He had lived a good life, although ultimately succumbed to death due to his compromised immune system. His family leaned on Cooke for guidance throughout his final days and funeral arrangements. As her sidekick, Cooke asked me to do as much or as little as I was comfortable with.

It was the first time I remember touching the body of someone deceased. The family had asked us to remove the ring off their loved one's hand, and I nodded to Cooke that I could do that. Admittedly, I was nervous about whether I would have any sort of visceral reaction to moving the hands and fingers of the body that laid in that casket. I gingerly lifted the left hand and wiggled the ring from his finger, all the while Cooke standing no more than two feet away, lending her signature presence that exuded confidence and support. More than anything, I remember feeling honored to do this task for the grieving family. I also remember, it wasn't nearly as frightening as I anticipated.

Then there was Father Hinds. I met him in his sunset years of life, when a significant stroke rendered him unable to live independently any longer. He moved into the long-term care unit of the continuum of care community where I worked in 2018. Fr. Hinds was wickedly smart, a well-read man who valued intellectually stimulating conversations. Although he was confined to his wheelchair after his stroke left him largely immobile, it was obvious he was a man of tall stature and had dined on many cuisine meals. His mouth had the signature droop following a stroke and at times he would involuntarily drool. Fr. Hinds had a gruff demeanor when he moved into our community and perhaps had always been that way. Yet, with very little time, I came to know two things about this man: First, his sharp sense of humor and big ole heart. Second was the struggle he was living – real time grief over the loss of his independence, and ongoing quandary of why he was still alive.

In my role as Director of Mission Integration & Spiritual Care, I was typically in private rooms or the corridors of the community interacting with residents and team members. The completion of mandated paperwork, email responses, and return calls to family members who had reached out often fell to the final hours of the day. I would do my best to quietly stow away in my office, in an attempt to get the tasks done without interruption. My office was behind the front desk, along with a half a dozen other offices in a hallway that was locked to anyone other than the leadership team. Often, I would be sending a final email at 6pm – desperately trying to leave so I could get some food and relief from a hefty day of serving so many when he would appear in my doorway.

Once positioned in his wheelchair, after being lifted from his bed with a Hoyer lift and two person assist, Fr. Hinds was mobile. Slow...but mobile! He would use his right hand to steer and shuffle his feet to traverse the long hallway from his unit to the front desk. Fr. Hinds would then *insist* on being let into the nucleus of offices behind the locked door. This would always occur after he had finished dinner, as I was doing my best to wrap up and essentially sneak out before being caught by another human who needed something...anything.

To be clear, I did not mind being "caught." Serving others is in my DNA. Yet, the days were long and often incredibly trying within the walls of an aging continuum of care. Between staffing shortages, colorful and contrasting personalities, resident's levels of care changes, and family expectations – it was a tricky equation to successfully solve. So, when Fr. Hinds feet would first appear in my doorway, then his knees, and next his half apathetic half proud and half ready to discuss the mysteries of life demeanor – well, I always had a heart sinking moment of realization that I would be there a while longer. Yes, Fr. Hinds was a full 150% even in this stage of his life! We would often talk for an hour or more, before I begged him to let me go for the evening. Sometimes he would let me push him back to his room, other times he chose to slowly shuffle himself to the 290 square feet that had become his final home.

Typically, within the first 60 seconds of his arrival, my attitude would shift. My heart would soften, as I was honored by Fr. Hinds' willingness to befriend me. I am a better human because of him. His presence allowed me to down shift from the hurried final push of the day to the point of leaning back and putting my feet up as we chatted. Our conversations spanned topics of global warming, his days as an active priest, theology in the modern world, books, how he was managing his decreasing independence, and how to improve the menu at our community. We cracked inappropriate jokes and dreamed of outrageous actions that would ruffle the feathers of others. The common theme through our conversations was mutual interest, respect, and love. I could hear and see his frustration with his dependance on others. Certainly, it is not part of the American dream to end up in a continuum of care in the golden years of one's life...yet here he was.

One evening as Fr. Hinds found his way back to my office, he came with a specific topic in mind. It required focus to gather exactly what he was saying at times, as his words slurred together due to the strokes. I was able to gather that a student he once taught, who had gone on to explore the world through his work for National Geographic, was returning to Cincinnati, Ohio to give an evening talk. It was scheduled for a weeknight at the local all-boys Catholic high school where Fr. Hinds had taught. I could tell he was excited, and it was clear he was lit up with the notion of getting to see this past student. With that dream in hand, we conjured up a plan. The team would shower and dress Fr. Hinds, I would get him into the community's lift van and drive him to attend the talk and visit a bit longer with his past student.

The day finally arrived, and we were on schedule, which was no small feat given the need for multiple caregivers to support bathing and dressing Fr. Hinds. It was always a bit stress-inducing to drive the facility lift van, given the size of the vehicle and precious cargo of residents on board. Tonight was different in that Fr. Hinds would be the only passenger on the bus. He had to be in the back, as that's where the straps were to properly fasten and secure his wheelchair for the ride. That just meant I had to holler in order to visit, as we set out on the 45-minute rush hour trek to the high school.

We had allotted plenty of time to ensure we would arrive early and get situated for the talk. Plans changed, however, when 20 minutes into the drive the engine started smoking. I was in the middle lane of a three-lane highway traveling north. Immediately, I felt flushed with panic. I shifted over to the right lane and reduced my speed, but the smoke pouring from the engine grew. In as calm of a voice as possible, I hollered back to Fr. Hinds that something was wrong...the engine was smoking! I then asked him what he thought we should do – knowing he was perfectly capable mentally, yet not so much physically. My mind raced wondering how the hell I was going to get him out of the bus and to safety. *What if it caught on fire?* The next exit was too far away, and the smoke was billowing! I put the hazard lights on and moved the community van through the thick, rush-hour traffic. I continued to tell Fr. Hinds the status, in an attempt to assure him we were going to get through this. I knew my running commentary was as much for myself as for him.

And then...Fr. Hinds started laughing. Body heaving, hysterically laughing. I wasn't there yet – I was still trying to manage through traffic and find a space on the shoulder of the road to pull off, all the while stressing that I didn't have a plan to get this wheelchair bound man off what I pictured as a flame engulfed vehicle. I hollered back, *"This isn't a laughing matter!"* in our classic banter, though then I found myself starting to laugh as well. Still panicked, but at least we were laughing together. In our sick humor, we acknowledged that if this was it, at least we'd be going out with a bang!

The long and short of this story is, I pulled the bus over on the shoulder. Help was deployed from two team members back at the community who came in their own vehicles – one for us to use and proceed to our evening plans, one for them to return to the community. Those two heroes assisted in getting Fr. Hinds out of the bus the hard way, because the vehicle was completely dead and the lift was not functional. We made it just in the nick of time to the talk, and returned to the community in one piece much later that night. The van was left abandoned on the side of the highway, to be addressed the next day during working hours. It was a grand adventure – a Make-A-Wish of sorts, for this man I had come to love. This man who had his independence stripped from him, yet still had a desire to be in community, to engage in an environmental conversation and rigor with a past student. It was worth it, even if I did gain a few gray hairs that day. We laughed a lot about blowing up the bus and talked about what a delight it was to be out for the night.

Several months later, Fr. Hinds died. It was a relief, as he continued to have small strokes which diminished his physical and mental capacity. His funeral was held at the Cathedral, with full pomp and circumstance on a perfect temperature, beautiful blue-sky day. It was a full Mass, incense, and sermon honoring Fr. Hind's contributions to the community. As his casket was wheeled out of the Cathedral, those who gathered to say our final goodbye filed out as the casket passed by our pew.

As I got to the grand doors, and stepped outside, I saw dozens of priests lined on both sides of the walkway, creating a path for Fr. Hinds' casket to pass through. The priests sang a final goodbye song, in all the richness of their baritone and tenor tones. I moved through the procession in awe. To this day, it gives me goosebumps. I can feel the power of how this man was sent off with love, after having lived so much life and so many deaths – the death of his independence, his voice, his strength.

Through these experiences, and others, I was awakened to the truth that death is not just about a loved one arriving at their final day and leaving this earth. Granted, unlike many of my peers, I have never been put off by wrinkles, smells, or any other thing that may accompany aging. People have often said, "*I could never do that*", or "*I'm glad there are people like you*" in relation to me working in the aging industry. Much like someone who is the "IT human" all day, every day, or the person who tends to animals, or finances, or cars. Or the teacher or day care provider who engages in ways that celebrate and guide little ones with such ease that it's obvious they are in the exact career they are meant to be in. It's inspiring to see a person's talents and passion come together in a way that serves others. That is me with aging individuals.

It has been through countless interactions with elders – sharing a meal, visiting at the hospital or rehabilitation facility, playing cards, baking together, sitting on a porch swing and watching the neighborhood happenings – that I've gleaned so much insight into the reality of death being both literal and figurative. These moments have opened my eyes and heart to a deeper understanding that death is truly part of the life cycle.

My innate love, curiosity, and ability to connect with elders allowed me to grow up embracing aging, death, and dying. Through countless experiences, I have observed and learned from others' transitions, letting go, and stepping into the next chapter of life.

Death has the ability to be both literal and figurative – and have the same monumental impact on a human. What a curious truth.

As my dad shared, *"Grief has become a surprise visitor. When you know somebody's very sick and going to die, psychologically, there's some preparation. The grief can be intense, yet you're waiting for it to happen."* He went on to share that through the years his understanding of grief evolved from being exclusively reserved for someone dying and has shown up far more frequently in the changing chapters of his life.

He is not alone in this experience and relationship with grief. Author and speaker, Heidi Priebe puts poignant words to the essence of grief being part of life. She says, *"To love someone long-term is to attend a thousand funerals of the people they used to be. The people they're too exhausted to be any longer. The people they don't recognize inside themselves anymore. The people they grew out of, the people they never ended up growing into. We so badly want the people we love to get their spark back when it burns out; to become speedily found when they are lost. But it is not our job to hold anyone accountable to the people they used to be. It is our job to travel with them between each version and to honor what emerges along the way. Sometimes it will be an even more luminescent flame. Sometimes it will be a flicker that disappears and temporarily floods the room with a perfect and necessary darkness."* (Priebe, H. *This Is Me Letting You Go*. Createspace Independent Publishing Platform, 2016)

As it turns out, grief is a companion on our journey through life – so the question is: How will we meet and engage with grief?

2

Grief Pioneers

We all have our own background and beliefs. Our experiences shape what we think about everything – life, work, play, emotions, family, community, finances, religion, politics, death and grief. Yes, I realize I just summarized the focus of humanity in the broad strokes of eleven categories. Certainly, there are far more, though you get my point. Our experiences shape our thoughts and how we approach any topic. I feel fortunate I was exposed early and relatively often, in order to embrace the idea that death truly is part of the cycle of life. As Valerie Harper says, *"We're all terminal; none of us are getting out of this alive."* My path has allowed me to experience death, dying, and grief with a spirit of intrigue, discovery, and growth.

Yet so many fear or avoid death at all costs. Rightfully so, as our brains are always busy scanning the environment to ensure we are free from danger. When we detect a threat, feel or recall a negative memory, or pick up cues that something unpleasant is about to happen, we retreat. This is the job of our amygdala, a tiny part of the brain that is responsible for identifying threats and triggering our parasympathetic nervous system that controls fight or flight. Since memories or feelings play into this reaction, it becomes an active pursuit to turn the tide of resistance – to notice and intentionally choose when the fight or flight mode is activated.

The fact that resistance to death and grief is baked into our operating systems is so important that it bears repeating and deeper consideration. Resistance is the tactic so often deployed as our brain strives to create safety and security. It appears when we don't perceive that we are safe, in control, or have a choice. What's interesting though, is while the brain is doing its complex work, it is blind to other truths. It does not decipher, nor does it understand that we are capable of experiencing hard things. It does not take into account the resiliency of our spirit or the capacity of our heart. And our brain does not accept that death and grief are going to happen to all of us, at some time, in some form or fashion.

Our brains are simply doing their job of avoiding danger. Meanwhile, we get to do the job of being human in all the moments. Although grieving may not make our Top 10 List of things we want to experience today, it is alive and well and we get to figure out ways to maneuver through grief that empower us to be our best selves.

This is when I turn to the pioneers before me, specifically researchers. Data has a powerful way of grounding me in what's real and tangible, so I can understand things that feel less so. When my brain is spinning out during a moment of grief, I am grateful for a deep breath and the reminder that wise leaders before me have been in similar situations and have created a path that's available if it serves me.

Enter Elisabeth Kübler-Ross. I first learned about this powerful pioneer and her five stages of grief during a psychology course on human development at Xavier University. Primed with my upbringing and exposure to death and dying, I was immediately enthralled by her work.

When Kübler-Ross published her first book, *On Death and Dying*, in 1969 it came from a rich history of personal and professional experiences. Both in Switzerland as a triplet, Elisabeth was a mere two pounds and was hospitalized within the first five years of life for pneumonia. It was then, at the age of five, that she first witnessed death. She was privy to other close deaths in her early years and established the belief that death was one of many phases of life and should be approached with dignity and peace. Yet, much like Kübler-Ross's experiences in the 1960s, many healthcare professionals are taught to fix, cure, and extend life. While this is a noble effort, avoiding the conversation and complex mental and emotional care that accompanies inevitable death is, I dare say, negligent.

Kübler-Ross attended medical school, practiced psychiatry, and worked closely with people who were dying. What she discovered through her work, listening, and professional lens were five stages of grief that a terminal patient processed through: denial, anger, bargain, depression, and acceptance. Her life's work was to *"break through the layer of professional denial that prohibited patients from airing their inner-most concerns."* (Kübler-Ross, E. *On Death and Dying.* Macmillan, 1969)

Upon diving into her work I discovered, with very little effort, that Kübler-Ross was at times frustrated at the interpretation of her stages of grief. Her original research was rooted in her direct care and work with terminally ill patients. The stages were created to offer greater awareness of what a *dying person* may experience. Our culture, while interested in avoiding the topic of death and dying, was equally desperate to cling onto any structure that made sense of the experience of loss and death. So, the stages of grief were applied to all types of loss, well beyond the original context in which they were created.

Kübler-Ross was also adamant that the stages of grief were not a linear process and that each individual experiences their own unique process of grief. Essentially, once her five stages of grief were so entrenched in the conversation of death and dying, she wanted to at least be clear that her work was not meant as a recipe to be followed with precision, rather served as a guide and offered deeper understanding to support a gentle experience of death, when possible.

It was the point about the origin of the five stages of grief that stopped me in my tracks so many years ago and has been bouncing around within me ever since. Kübler-Ross was at the bedside of terminally ill patients. She outlined and detailed the stages of denial, anger, bargaining, depression, and acceptance from the lens of someone who was dying. *The stages of grief were not originally meant to be for survivors or for everyday life.* Yet, her work was needed. Desperately.

I equate this to the moments when all I have available is a knife to awkwardly attempt to unscrew a Phillips screw. It's not ideal, but it works. Granted, it's rather cumbersome and either tweaks the end of the knife or grazes my fingertip or takes an inordinate amount of time compared to having an actual Philips screwdriver. But we adapt, right? Sometimes we don't have the best tool, so we make do with what we have. That is what we have done with Kübler-Ross's Stages of Grief. We've taken something that was researched and created for a specific subset and applied it to all. Much like the knife clumsily attempting to accomplish what I need, so too are the stages of grief applied to humans living everyday life.

There have been many more who have contributed to our understanding of grief. When I was 34, I came upon *The Grief Recovery Handbook*, a beautifully powerful book and process created by John James and Russell Friedmann. As often is the case, we find what we need in the moment. I was living one of the darkest death experiences I had ever encountered – divorce. A death of hopes, dreams, and expectations. Divorce: An ending no one ever believes will happen when you are in the throes of the early stages of love and excitement.

From the outside, and so many years later, it was obvious our marriage was not going to work. I should have more closely considered the red flag that I was his third wife, and he was actively engaged in his addiction. From a more nuanced perspective, we were interwoven in a codependency that was unwell. He was seeking to fill a void of acceptance and love that was rooted in a feeling of abandonment wrapped within his story of origin. I was seeking acceptance and love rooted in self-loathing and the stories of unworthiness I had compiled for myself through the years. He was addicted to alcohol and then narcotics. I was the provider, caregiver, and medical advocate. Our own unacknowledged, uncared for woundedness prevented us from showing up as a partner for the other. So, on our third anniversary we agreed any form of celebrating would be dishonest and perfunctory. A year and some change later, our divorce was final, and I was in a dark place of grief.

Fortunately, I was in the field of healthcare, so I was surrounded by exceptionally versed professionals who could point me toward support. I landed in a grief group hosted at a local hospice. It was a structured process for a specific number of weeks built around *The Grief Recovery Handbook*. I went through the steps with integrity, each week reading and doing my homework with specific tasks around the experience of grief I was focusing on. The goal was to create completion. At the start of the support group, I never could have imagined that feeling complete would be possible based on how deeply I hurt from my divorce. Yet, within eight weeks, I was able to breathe deeply again and pop my head up, much like Punxsutawney Phil on Ground Hog Day – except I was ready to be among the living again.

The Grief Recovery Method saved me. To this day, I recommend this book and process to anyone experiencing grief. At its best, the intention is to work through the process laid out in the handbook and allow yourself to be witnessed by another person, or a group. They are not coaching or guiding you, rather simply hearing you in each step of the journey to completion of grief. I have always appreciated and resonated with the analogy provided by a trainer during a Grief Recovery certification I pursued in 2013. The idea presented was as follows:

Imagine you accidentally slip, fall, and break your leg while out running errands. Would you go get medical treatment, repair the break, do therapy, and regain full functionality of your leg? Or would you get up and proceed without treatment or therapy, as if nothing ever happened? In this second scenario, at the very least you spend the rest of your life with a limp.

No one can argue that the first option is the one most people choose. However, when your heart breaks, you may not be as clear about what needs to be done to heal it. So often we take the second option, proceeding through life with a crippled heart. We are resilient...to an extent. Too often we are quick to address physical ailments while brushing emotional ailments under the rug. This does not serve anyone.

I felt incredibly equipped between Kübler-Ross's stages of grief and the actionable steps of James' and Friedman's Grief Recovery Method...so much so that I attended an intensive training and became certified in the Grief Recovery Method. I purchased the book for countless individuals, I worked the process for myself over and over again to create completion around the grief of my divorce, various deaths in my life, jobs that I didn't get, boyfriends that didn't stick – really the whole spectrum of losses that created little breaks in my heart.

Completion energy is an interesting concept when it comes to grief. It doesn't make the loss disappear or change the course of history. It's not meant to do either of those. The intention of completion energy is to fully tend to the grief in order to have a heart (and let's go ahead and add in body, mind, and spirit) that can proceed in life even after grief strikes. The gift of completion energy is to offer time and space to feel, process, and say the word "*goodbye*", which signals to our brains that a phase of a relationship, situation, or dream is done.

Perhaps an example will highlight the gift of completion energy. The divorce that I mentioned was my first marriage. Yes, you read the right, "first marriage." I realize the goal is to only get married once and create a lifetime together, forever and always. Yet, that was not the case for me. Although we had known each other for 14 years, our marriage only represented three of those years. By the time our divorce was final I was a single 34-year-old who had a broken heart that desperately wanted to find love. So, I did all the things, which is to say all the dating apps. Sure, I was open to friends introducing me to someone – that happened a few times. Yet, nothing really stuck. I kissed a lot of frogs and a few potential princes over the course of eight years.

And then I went on my last first date. I went into the date relatively indifferent – that's what years' worth of first dates can do to a person! I also went in completely authentic because I was finally at the point of being comfortable enough with myself to know I had nothing to lose and that the guy was going to need to impress me before I offered the effort to impress him. On December 20, 2020 at 8pm Patrick and I met at the statue of Mr. Roebling on the Kentucky side of the Ohio River. It was a cold, dark Tuesday in the middle of a global pandemic, so an outside walk with hot toddies after work was the solution. That walk lasted five hours, covered a whole host of topics, and laid out each of our non-negotiables. We've not left each other's side since.

This isn't about our love story though; it's about completion energy, so let me tell another facet of this story.

We were very intentional throughout our dating. As adults in our forties, we were clear we wanted to take our time and enjoy the early phase of euphoric, eros love. Then settle into a deeper commitment, pragma love. And of course, the most comfortable love with one another. We dated a full year before I was officially introduced to Patrick's kids. We got engaged on our fourth anniversary. But it was about two and a half years in that I had a moment.

I remember it vividly. It was a weekend, early in the spring. We were doing some yard work at my house. Patrick was removing debris from the drains in my driveway and moving around the yard picking up various areas. I was in the garage sweeping.

I distinctly recall feeling an unshakable agitation. There was no real reason I could identify feeling this way. Yet, as Patrick and I had a conversation in the midst of doing yard work together, the feeling kept growing. Initially I quietly scolded myself for feeling how I felt and especially for directing it at my man who was so generously helping clean up my yard. Next, I tried to shake it off, only to have the effect of growing the feeling. So, as Patrick was on the other side of the yard, I stopped to really take account of what was wrong with me. I wasn't hungry. I wasn't hormonal. There was nothing going on with Patrick and me that had my feathers ruffled.

And suddenly, it occurred to me! In the midst of working together with the man I chose to do life with; I was grieving my single life! Over two years into a quite amazing relationship, the feeling of grief reared its head in the form of unexplainable agitation. The instant I identified this for myself; it began to subside. The feelings softened and within just a few minutes, I assessed that missing the single life was not an indication that I needed to return to it, rather a moment of grieving .... letting go.

Now, I fully recognize this was some late processing. Two and a half years into the relationship and I was just getting that I would no longer have the perks that accompany complete independence? Yeah, sometimes grief works that way, doesn't it? We can't understand or plan all the ways letting go of one thing is going to affect us. I needed to have that moment in the garage to reflect on how awesome it was to be single and simultaneously feel the joy and active commitment to the relationship I was creating with Patrick. It shook me up for a minute, quite honestly. For a brief moment, I questioned whether these feelings were telling me to cut bait and move on. Fortunately, I allowed the feelings to flow and recognized there were two things at play: Choice and Grief. I had the choice to be coupled or single, and whichever one I chose would result in grief.

Just as suddenly as the realization arrived, so did the choice. I wanted this ever-evolving relationship with Patrick. So, I got to grieve my carefree, single sailing life. I remember standing in the garage with a silly smile – never could I have anticipated grieving being single! All those years of heart-longing dating had come to an end more than two years prior. Yet, when we make room for one thing we often must say goodbye to another. I had my completion moment with being single in the garage that day. I literally said, *"Goodbye single life"* and went and told Patrick about the moment I had just had – more for my own processing than anything.

Saying *"goodbye"* is radically important for completion energy, in both figurative and literal death experiences. This is not an immediate step, but rather *The Grief Recovery Handbook* offers a gentle process to move you to the place where you can write and speak these words that create some relief.

I recall guiding a precious friend to this step a year after the death of her son, August. Candace had spent the year in deep grief after her son was born premature and lived four powerful days before passing away. She found herself in a place of need to create some completion energy, which she did in a letter to her son:

Dear August,

I apologize for living a stressful schedule while I was pregnant. I apologize for continuing to run even when you were asking me to slow down. I apologize for waiting so long to go to the hospital when I was in labor. I apologize for making a rash decision about unplugging the machines. I was selfish. I didn't want to feel more pain. I killed you. I apologize for taking your life. I forgive you for pushing so hard to be born. I forgive you for giving up. I forgive you for leaving me, August.

I want you to know that I think about you every day. I love you, every day you are always on my mind and heart. I want you to know how special you are to me and to your family, how much you taught us and continue to teach us.

August, I love you.
I miss you.
Goodbye.

Love,
Mommy

This goodbye did not solve anything. It did, however, shift the heavy blanket of grief that had been upon her. To this day, tears flow as Candace rereads this letter. And...she finds herself in an ever-evolving relationship with grief versus being stuck.

Completion energy opens up space. It allows flow – some things in, some things out. Which brings to mind the cycle of the seasons, or scripture that tells us there is a time for everything, or the sun and moon rising and setting. We experience completion energy more than we know each and every day, in both big and little ways. The power comes when we truly get present and notice the completion moments. It's as if we are closing some doors and opening others, in order to move forward through the days and years of our lives.

The Grief Recovery Handbook is a powerful tool. I will always be a champion of this process. It is thorough and simple, all at once. It is for any and all moments of loss in life – death of a loved one or pet, divorce, loss of a job, accident, health diagnosis, and on and on. Please seek this resource out for yourself or find a local group and participate in a facilitated process: griefrecoverymethod.com

As our brains do their job of protecting us when grief strikes, there is also a notion of appropriate grief. My mentor and clinical expert, Tammy Miller-Ploetz, introduced me to this concept. While there is some degree of grief when a person dies, our minds more readily categorize the 95-year-old who passes peacefully in her sleep as appropriate grief, compared to the 32-year-old with four children who is diagnosed with stage four cancer and has a quick death. This second example is so difficult to grapple with – it's a jolt to our system and there's no way to make sense of it in our minds. A quick and unexpected death often leaves the living feeling disenfranchised. This is what we call inappropriate death. How and when a person dies, whether it was witnessed or not, and the timing all play into whether it gets categorized in our minds as appropriate or inappropriate.

Even outside of literal death, our brains play such an integral part in our experiences of grief. A friend reflected on her experience of sending her first born off to college. "*I naturally stepped into my head more than my heart, which I feel like we do in many situations of grief. I got really involved in the logistics and mechanics of what had to be done as a way of keeping myself busy and avoiding grief. I remember the only time I had a true heart moment of grief was after I took her to school and we had jumped through all the hoops and she was settled into her room; I came back to her room in our house. As I stripped her bed, I finally sat down and cried.*"

Lindsey's insights are clear in the midst of preparing her second child for college. This time around, she is giving herself more room and grace to feel it all as they experience the "lasts" and "firsts." She is allowing herself to move from living only in her head to sinking into her heart in the process of witnessing her children extend their wings.

Pursuing moments of appropriate death looks like having conversations with our loved ones or being guided through a life review that creates posterity and legacy. Honoring our brain's brilliant functioning as well as our heart's longing looks like slowing down and creating space for being as much as doing. And exploring the research, concepts, and wisdom set forth by countless pioneers in the realm of grief is right and important work for all of us. Some of those grief pioneers include David Kessler, a friend and protégé of Kübler-Ross, who added a Sixth Stage of Grief: Finding Meaning. Alan Wolfelt founded the Center for Loss & Life Transition. Frances Weller specializes in grief work, shame, and addiction. Even Anderson Cooper has created a space to vulnerably talk about grief. These are not the only ones, rather a small taste for anyone interested in delving deeper. I dare say it's a topic we could all benefit from exploring.

Which brings me back to Elisabeth Kübler-Ross. For years, I've felt profound gratitude and admiration for her work. While I have never had a terminal prognosis, I have had cancer twice. I have sat by the bedside of others dying. I have witnessed – within myself and others – the process of death, dying, and grief. Which is the path to this book. One that I hope builds upon Elisabeth Kübler-Ross's five stages of grief. She was a pioneer. If I had met her, I suspect she would want her work to go on...to grow and develop further.

3

Introducing The 5 Powers of Grief

It was the perfect recipe: attending funerals, learning about Elisabeth Kübler Ross' five stages of grief, living my own moments of loss, The Grief Recovery Method, and a desire to evolve the way our culture views death and loss. With these ingredients blended, my own understanding of grief began to surface.

The 5 Powers of Grief incorporate the lessons I have lived and witnessed so far. At the risk of repeating myself, my intention is to evolve our understanding and language to reflect the role grief plays in our lives. My dream is to fundamentally shift how we engage with grief, to support growth.

Truth be told, I'm not too concerned about repeating myself. Science shows that in the noisy world we live in, repetition learning increases processing fluency and memory. (Zhan, Lexia et al. "Effects of Repetition Learning on Associative Recognition Over Time: Role of the Hippocampus and Prefrontal Cortex." *Frontiers in human neuroscience* vol. 12 277. 11 Jul. 2018, doi:10.3389/fnhum.2018.00277) Don't be surprised if I continue to sprinkle my intention throughout this book.

I grappled for some time before landing on calling these The 5 Powers of Grief. Initially, I considered calling them cycles or seasons – both words that offer the essence of movement. I believe grief is that way, it bends and swirls within us, showing up in different moments and in different ways. Yet, there was something that didn't quite land for me with those words.

It was while getting ready for work in the early months of 2025 that I had a breakthrough. At this point, the hairs on the nape of my neck and around my ears had been trimmed once since the regrowth from being bald. The journey of growing hair – and so many other chemotherapy impacts – is an interesting process and powerful experience of grief.

In my early twenties, while living in Anchorage, Alaska I let a friend cut all of my hair to a tussled two inches. I had never considered going all the way down to bald though! I had too many untrue stories in my head about my appearance, and my hair was one tool at the ready that allowed me to feel pretty...most days.

So, it felt distressing when my hair started coming out in clumps three weeks after my first chemotherapy treatment – right on schedule with what my gentle oncologist had said would happen. For me, a slow departure of my shoulder length hair would be more excruciating than taking control. As my brain panicked, I decided to have my partner shave my head.

On Labor Day 2023, Patrick lovingly buzzed me down to bald and then took the clippers and buzzed his own head in an act of solidarity. Staring in the mirror at the radically white pigment of my bald scalp, I became immediately aware that my hair had been serving as a security blanket unbeknownst to me all this time. Amazingly, this terrifying reality of being seen in such a raw and real way subsided within an hour of Patrick shaving my head. Just as I had never thought I could be bald, I never knew transformation could be equally easy. The factor present in allowing for this "easy" transformation resided in allowing myself to break open. We'll revisit that notion in Chapter Seven.

Fast forward a year. Just as I had never fathomed baldness, similarly I did not anticipate the burdensome feeling that accompanied regrowing my hair. This is actually the first time I am publicly confessing this truth. After rocking out being bald for six months, I knew the stubble...then shag...then awkward lengths of locks were all signs of my body working and recalibrating into wellness again. I knew others were in the throes of their own trials, tribulations, and treatments so who was I to complain about my hair regrowing? That said, there were many parts of the return to wellness that stirred my grief – and continue to do so. Eyelashes that have never fully regrown or that routinely show up in my eyes like tiny little splinters. Nails that break and split from the hormonal imbalance created by medically induced menopause. Eyes that remain chronically dry 18 months after the last dose of chemotherapy was pumped into my veins through the port in my chest. Shifted expectations of myself by myself and others. The remnants of breast cancer – my most radical interruption in life to date – were and are still so very alive. I share all of this not from a victim mentality, rather to cast light on my journey...which I suspect many can relate to.

Which brings me back to early 2025, standing in front of the mirror getting ready. It was a moment of discernment on what to call the ideas I was so committed to sharing with others as a way of understanding, honoring, and moving with and through our individual and collective grief. The thought bolted through my mind to call these five "things" The Powers of Grief. My ego perked up for a quick second and smiled at the connection to my last name. Quickly though, my mind summoned Dr. Alois Alzheimer, Lou Gehrig, Robert Graves, and Hakaru Hashimoto. All of these humans had something named after them, however, all are unwanted conditions or diseases. My inner dialogue discerned that if I was ever going to have something named after me, I did not want it to be a disease. Instead, I would want it to be something that served others.

This was far greater than an ego moment. I've come to recognize when ideas pop into my head or heart, they are most often Godwinks. Call it what you will – the Universe showing up, God speaking to my heart, having an experience higher and greater than myself – when ideas flow seemingly out of the blue, I have learned to listen and sit with those thoughts a bit.

As I spent some time reflecting on naming these ideas The 5 Powers of Grief, it felt good. In pursuing the etymology of the word *"power"* I found it comes from the Latin word *"potis"* which means powerful. The infinitive form of the word is *"potere"* which means *"to be able."*

Yes! To be able. That is at the core of the ideas within this book! To be able – to be interrupted, to feel it all, to hold onto the past, to break free of that hold, and to recreate ourselves in the here and now from all the pieces of what we were and what we can be. That is the purest and most beautiful form of power, in my opinion. Not skewed by being more than another, rather being present to self as the moments of life refine us.

If you've never considered yourself to be powerful, or if you feel resistant to the word, I encourage you to explore further.

1. Sit with the root of the word: To be able.

2. Reflect on your life and all the moments you have been able – able to laugh, cry, walk, run, rest, love, grieve. You being able IS you being powerful!

I actually believe resistance can teach us something new about ourselves or others. Resistance can be a primal cue to be alert and aware, it can be a reflection of our own thoughts and beliefs, or it can be an invitation to stretch out of our comfort zone. In other words, resistance can be the proverbial rumble strip when we veer too close to danger, a non-threatening moment of noticing self-proclaimed limitations, or a signal that you're about to grow!

Ultimately, whatever your experience with the word power may be, I implore you to give it a chance. Our roots of humanity are intertwined with power – the kind that reminds us we are able. Just because power has been twisted and contorted in our world does not mean that has to ring true in our personal relationship with power. Perhaps coming home to ourselves and getting familiar and accessing our power is part of the evolution and revolution that is required here and now. If grappling with the word power is stretchy for you, please accept my gratitude for being open.

So, without further ado, these are The 5 Powers of Grief based on my studies, my experiences, and my heart:

1. The Interruption
2. Flow of Feelings
3. Holding
4. Breaking
5. Re-Membering

I want to pause here and give you a moment to take in the names of The 5 Powers of Grief I am sharing. Take a moment to reread these. Notice your reactions.

What comes up?

Are you eager...angry...apprehensive?

Are you curious...annoyed...tired?

Can you let yourself simply be?

Can you sit with whatever is coming up?

~~~~~

I have a circle of wise women in my life. One of them said to me, "*Grief comes in waves. A lot of times, it knocks you over, like waves crashing on a beach. Sometimes it's fun, sometimes you're like 'ok, that one pummeled me!' and sometimes you get taken under by it.*"

Grief does feel heavy so very often. By integrating the language of The 5 Powers of Grief, is it possible for grief to also be a tender companion? Is there more to grief than heaviness and being taken under?

In the chapters that follow, I will spend time unpacking each Power of Grief. We'll explore together and invite this new perspective as it pertains to grief. As we begin, I would like to offer a few considerations:

Grief is cyclical and an everyday process. Sometimes we feel it more deeply, other times we flow with it.

Babysitting was my first job growing up. I was the oldest of nearly two dozen cousins and my parents were open to opportunities in our community where my sister and I could spread our wings and step into the role of babysitting. Babies have always been my preference. I didn't mind changing diapers or trying to soothe their crying...I was easily wrapped up in their sheer presence. Toddlers – well, I suppose I subscribed to the terrible twos stereotype. Those were rough babysitting experiences for me: the all-out fighting against bedtime – tears and tantrums despite being so exhausted. What I didn't recognize then was resistance to the daily cycle: wake, eat, poop, play, sleep... and repeat. And every night there was a struggle to give into sleep. The kiddos did not want to let go of the day. They didn't want to give in. I now see that this is the perfect example of grief showing up in everyday life.

Grief is letting go of one thing to make room for something else.

Although my first marriage was relatively brief, finally letting it go was a delayed process. Releasing the hopes and dreams I had for my marriage was hard. There were many moments of denial, bargaining, and anger – all the while holding onto something that was not well. When I finally said the words and took the steps of divorce, it felt as if the whole world was crumbling in on me. I knew, of course, that life would go on...however, I could not see the path. It was a dark, lonely, cold period of life with literal aching of my heart. I guess what I see now, so many years later, is that I needed to let go of what I thought was true and healthy love to make room for an even greater love. It started with authentic self-love, and from there opened doors to romantic love again. It wasn't immediate. I had to heal after such a deep and dark letting go. Yet, without letting go of my marriage, I know I would not have been open to the life and relationship I have now.

Grief is transition.

If grief is letting go of one thing to make room for another, and an everyday process, doesn't that mean that grief is transition? Playing with that idea has opened my mind and heart to the experience of grief. The toddler resisting giving into another day being over as signified by bedtime. Sending a pet over the rainbow bridge to perhaps welcome another later. Ending the marriage. Packing up and moving into the college dorm...or packing up and moving out of the college dorm. Watching your 16-year-old drive away in the car on their own for the first time. Onboarding at a new job. Holding the hand of your loved one as they transition out of this life. Grief is what occurs in the midst of transition.

Grief is ultimately a very personal journey – no two people experience it the same, and even the same person may have radically different experiences of grief throughout their life. With that in mind, I will remind you that if you find yourself getting tight or resisting the message within this book – set it down. Breathe. Give yourself some time and space.

I also ask you to be as open as possible. Some of my musings may seem unrealistic or stretchy at first, yet with a heart of acceptance, these same ideas may be what support you in unlocking your own healing...your grief may become a catalyst for growth simply by letting a new way of facing it into your thoughts and heart.

4

The Interruption

*The Interruption: A disruption that demands
our attention and brings grief, whether positive
(graduation, marriage) or painful (divorce, death).*

Grief begins with an interruption.

Beep beep beep beep...

Beeeeeeep...beep beep beep beep...beeeeeep....

**We interrupt your regularly scheduled programming
to bring you this breaking news!**

We've all likely heard this interruption while watching tv or listening to the radio. Perhaps it's the monthly siren to test the emergency communication systems of your hometown, or maybe there is breaking news to be communicated. The beeping catches our attention, it is unexpected. Have you ever paused to notice though, we tap into whatever the issue may be for a brief moment and then, and even during the prescribed message of the interruption, we return to our regularly scheduled programming. Meaning, we turn the channel or proceed with our task...we get back to our life and routines of the moment.

Interruptions. A break of continuity. Something that pauses or halts the flow we are in.

All throughout life, we experience little and big interruptions. We call them different things – failing, falling, being denied, accidents, mistakes, wrong turns, choices. Yet, at the core they are interruptions to the path and pattern we created and are living. These little and big interruptions either stop us in our tracks or send us quickly spiraling down a different path.

Reflect for a moment on your life. Perhaps it has some, or all, of these components:

You were born. You were loved by your family – adopted or blood.

You experienced some moments of turmoil and tension between the adults in your home, or stress over homework that was more complicated than you knew how to manage. You tried out for sports, band, honor societies, debate team. You excelled at times and were not selected other times. You felt this deeply, yet you continued on.

You made it through high school and decided to get a job or continue more schooling. In the midst of that process, you were rejected a few times and had to keep applying...keep seeking where you would land.

You arrived, wherever "arriving" was for you – a job, a neighborhood, a partnership, a dream. As you carried on from this place that you sought out for so long, you happened upon a new relationship, or a layoff. You got pregnant or had a chance to buy a house. You adopted a puppy or dealt with the bottom of the hot water heater rusting away.

And life continued through it all. The years passed and you became more seasoned in all areas of life.

Then someone died. Or you found yourself as an empty nester. Or you decided to downsize your home. Again, life continued. At some point, you retired from the work you were doing and found yourself in a whole new rhythm of life. You aged, perhaps well...perhaps full of dis-ease.

This is your life. Both simple and complex.

All of this is the process of life. We get in a groove, we create and follow a path, we fall and get up, we succeed and proceed. Yet notice – there are little and big interruptions that happen at every age and stage of life. Not getting first seat in band. Not being selected for the sports team. Not being admitted to the college. Not getting the scholarship you applied for. Not getting the job you applied for. Getting pulled over for speeding. Getting married and leaving behind the routines of single life. A miscarriage. The birth of a baby that comes with lack of sleep and shifted routines. A marriage that doesn't last. A health diagnosis that comes out of left field. A retirement – chosen or forced. A trip that is cancelled or one that is a last-minute addition. A conversation hijacked by another. A dead water heater, an egg broken on the floor, a stubbed toe. A death.

The versatility of this list is intentional. From a stubbed toe to a death, interruptions happen every day. What may be a small interruption to you may be massive to me, or vice versa. Ultimately, an interruption breaks the flow we've created and anticipated for ourselves. We establish as many efficiencies as possible to manage the magnitude of responsibilities in our lives. When something goes off course, it is an interruption. Can you see why the broken egg or a broken leg can both be categorized as an interruption?

Moreover, can you see that an interruption may actually be an illumination to call us back to center, to wake us up, to break us free from living in autopilot mode?

Think of it this way, an interruption shocks us out of our current systems. It snaps a finger and breaks the daze that we're living within. An interruption moves us out of our brain into our body. Depending on the type of interruption, there may be a surge of hormones – adrenaline, cortisol, dopamine.

These create sweaty palms, racing heart rhythms, and wide eyes – all bodily awareness and attention we did not have prior to the interruption. This is why I propose we look at this first Power of Grief as illumination, shedding light where it was not. Creating a pause to go within and get a read on how you are in relation to the new information – The Interruption. Although an interruption may be frustrating or painful, it offers an opportunity to go within – a self-check of sorts – offering a greater illumination and awareness of what I am, how I am, where I am and what's going on with and for me.

The heavy side of interruptions is the realization that you may be living your life on autopilot. Granted, operating from autopilot has benefits and barriers. The benefits are ease and efficiency, to "handle" all the things you are responsible for. The barriers are becoming *human doings* rather than *human beings*! When we sink into autopilot, we often disconnect from our humanity as well as the heart and deeper why of what we are doing. While usually not welcome, an interruption calls us back to our humanity. It causes us to pause and get present – inclusive of whatever may follow. That is the power of The Interruption... reengaging in life for a moment, a chapter, a season of time.

Interruptions disrupt us – mentally, physically, emotionally, and spiritually. Like stressors, interruptions can be labeled as positive or negative. While I do not subscribe to such a binary, simplistic view of interruptions, I also do not discount how hard and challenging interruptions can be to our life. I've lived them... you've lived them...I feel confident we can hold space for how heavy, sad, and dull some of life's interruptions have made us feel.

I hope we can also hold space for the other side of the coin – the excitement, anticipation, and joy some of life's interruptions bring. Because much like stressors, interruptions come in all shapes, sizes, and moments. Below are some categories and examples of interruptions for your consideration. My invitation is for you to notice how you think and feel about each of these. Are you resistant? Can you relate? Do you have other examples come to mind and heart? When you stop and reflect, are you aligned that these are things that break your routine cadence of life?

Personal Health & Well-Being Interruptions
- Breaking a bone
- A medical diagnosis
- New or regained abilities – Either relearning how to move and operate after a physical issue or learning how to adapt and integrate a newly established skill
- Post-partum
- Perimenopause and Menopause
- The psychological drain of being a care partner
- An addiction or mental health dynamic that alters who a person is
- The gradual decline and loss through Alzheimer's disease and recognizing the person you once knew is no longer the same
- Your three-year-old not yet talking initially not a problem, but now it is and all the testing and interventions to figure out what is going on
- *(add your own here...)*
- ...
- ...

Vocation/Professional Interruptions
- Failing a test
- Passing a test
- Graduating from college
- Starting a new job
- Being laid off
- Being fired
- Retiring
- Having a new task or project assigned to you
- *(add your own here...)*
- ...
- ...

Financial/Material Interruptions
- Water, electricity, wifi going out or being turned off
- Being in debt
- New expenses – Whether planned or unplanned, like car problems, college tuition, a high heat bill that interrupts your standard financial plan
- Newfound resources – Winning the lottery or receiving a gift that enables you to relook at your situation or make different decisions
- *(add your own here...)*
- ...
- ...

Emotional Interruptions
- Death of a loved one – Including, but not limited to family, friends, pets, close and distant connections, community leaders
- Divorce
- Receiving negative feedback which can send a person into a place of rumination
- Receiving a compliment which can positively stop a person in their track
- Letting go of a dream
- Pursuing a dream which causes one to alter how they manage their resources of time, energy, money to accomplish the dream
- Ambiguous loss – Life not going as planned or something not coming to fruition the way you thought it would
- A negative feeling taking root in a child's mind early on after a cutting criticism from their parent
- Losing a favorite, irreplaceable stuffed animal as a child
- Loss of one's identity and continual transformation from individual to pregnant person, to mom of a new human

- A midlife crisis – Which I believe is more accurately named Midlife Calm, the title of a book I authored that may be of interest as you explore different ways of perceiving moments
- *(add your own here...)*
- ...
- ...

Communal Interruptions
- A global pandemic
- Riots and looting
- Shootings at schools and in the streets
- New legislation
- Loss of friends and community as a result of embracing your own identity
- Parades and road closures
- *(add your own here...)*
- ...
- ...

With all these examples of interruptions, it's no wonder we feel heavy at times! There's an impact on us when our groove is altered.

I also acknowledge that there is a difference between grief and trauma. My sage mentor and precious friend, Candace shared this reality from her experience of childbirth and then child death. *"Separating grief from trauma has been really important for me. It was a process to conceive, carry, deliver, parent, and lose August. There was a lot of trauma associated with being in triage eight times in six weeks...every time thinking my baby had died. I was so wrapped up in the trauma my own body had experienced that I wasn't even able to access grief for some period of time."*

Candace's wisdom, four years after her son August died,

speaks to the added complexity when trauma is involved in grief. While this book does not delve into trauma, it felt too important to forgo mentioning. I highly encourage seeking professional counsel and support for anyone facing trauma with grief.

Returning to the conversation of The Interruption, have you ever stopped to consider if we did not have interruptions? We would continue on the path we are on. Think about that for a moment. Just continuing on...

In some ways it sounds lovely! Smooth sailing, mindless wandering, free of interruptions – sign me up! We absolutely all get to have moments like this. Yet, with eyes wide open, a life without any alterations also sounds bland. As humans we seek some degree of routine as well as spontaneity. Without some course corrections in my life, I would be in a very different place. While that's not good or bad, proceeding on autopilot reflects my brain running the show and operating from seeking safety over new opportunities, or routine over adventure. I would assert that an interruption, for whatever pain or grief it brings, can also be what wakes us up and invites us into active participation.

All of this means, in addition to the heaviness of living life in autopilot – simply going through the motions – there are other possibilities. The power of The Interruption is becoming engaged. And if shifting from autopilot to engaged is too far of a leap, the neutral option with The Interruption is to practice gentle awareness and curiosity.

Interruptions are going to happen in life. Often. Some, we see coming, and some take us off guard. How we choose to interact with The Interruption makes all the difference. In Chapter 10, I share images to help illustrate these ideas. Additionally, I offer questions to explore as you acquaint yourself with The 5 Powers of Grief. These are here to support us all in moving between the heaviness and power that is within grief.

5

Flow of Feelings

Flow of Feelings: A flood of emotions swirl in response to the Interruption. Everything from denial, anger, and sadness to acceptance, excitement, and anticipation.

Through my own experiences of grief and witnessing others, I believe the second Power of Grief is where Kübler-Ross's stages of grief reside. Flow of Feelings is just that – the rush of emotions that flood in after The Interruption.

There are three primary reasons why it is so easy to feel consumed by Flow of Feelings. First, the feelings that accompany an interruption are typically categorized as undesirable feelings. Fear, anger, frustration, sadness, loneliness, and confusion – to name a few. Even though there can be other feelings wrapped in as well, the ones noted as negative seem to drown out everything else. Simply put, no one *likes* feeling these things, yet there is value to be gleaned from experiencing these emotions.

Second, and likely because we are so averse to the feelings that get stirred up by an interruption, we are unfamiliar with what to do with them. It's normal to be hesitant and even to shy away from unfamiliar things that seem prickly. Do we want to be caught crying in public? Do we want to be distracted in a meeting due to a flow of feelings? Do we want to have an unexpected outburst of anger? Typically speaking, most people do not want to show up in any of these ways. So, while the feelings are big and intense within, when we don't know what to do with them, we often turn to hiding or masking until we have a moment alone.

Which leads to the third reason it is so easy to feel consumed by Flow of Feelings. Our society is fast paced, success oriented, and has not adopted a widespread understanding, language, or rituals around grief or Flow of Feelings. As a result, we are all left to our own devices. When you are juggling everyday stressors and pressure to fulfill commitments and responsibilities, only to have an interruption pop up...well, it's understandable that you may not have the wherewithal to ask for what you need or carve out space that you can actually feel the feels.

And so, the nasty cycle of

I don't have time for this
 I don't even know how to get through this
  I hate feeling this way
   I will focus on the things I know how to do
    I feel even more alone and sad

                    perpetuates.

This is when Flow of Feelings feels heavy. As we experience the heavy side of Flow of Feelings, it is easy for the cascade of feelings to grow into feeling isolated, lonely, depressed, afraid, and a whole host of other feelings. Although it has been many years since I earned my degrees and practiced clinical social work, the Diagnostic and Statistical Manual of Mental Disorders, 5th Edition (DSM-5) is a significant piece of literature that details mental illnesses. Depression is one of many mental health disorders that is real and should be monitored and treated by a physician or supported by a counselor. That said, I also have long wondered if we are a culture that fears *feeling* depressed, or low in spirits. It strikes me that similar to grief, our culture is not very versed with feelings that dip low and are heavy. We avoid feeling the heaviness.

This is real. And it is not just you. This is a societal issue and at the core of why I am writing this book. I believe we have an epidemic of unresolved grief. While we can name, label, and write extensive (and necessary) mental health disorder books and research, what we have not done well yet is to be present to our grief – personally and communally. Attention to our emotions, especially grief related feelings, is as vitally important and plays into an understanding of our mental health.

While interviewing people about their experiences of grief, they shared, *"grief shakes your confidence"* and *"I've had to really wrestle with differentiating between my thoughts and feelings."* It's tricky, because some humans have been raised with the belief that someone, somewhere is worse off than you, or that there is no time for feelings...we have to keep focused on the goal and forge ahead, regardless of your feelings. Much like Kübler-Ross explained, The Powers of Grief are not a linear process. What has been largely consistent in middle class, Caucasian society, however, has been an unwitting commitment to the heavy side of grief. While other cultures have language and rituals to support their community in moving from the heavy to the powerful aspects of grief, we have remained largely stagnant.

Yet, there are clues all around to learn from - the transition from winter to spring or fall to winter can be fast or prolonged if you live in the Midwest. A sunset that casts radiant colors on the horizon for hours or simply sinks away without much ado. The moon, the waves, the newly hatched birds learning to fly, the bear awakening from hibernation all happen in their own time. Nature does not follow a manufactured experience of checking off the boxes. When you become too hurried in your personal process of grief, like when you feel consumed by your Flow of Feelings, that is when you get to remember there is both a neutral and powerful option of how you engage. Those options are gentle awareness and curiosity or bearing witness.

My hope is for your heart to feel a little understood as you read this book. And for you to have a deeper understanding that the heaviness you may feel during the second Power of Grief actually has another side to it. The power within Flow of Feelings is to bear witness. This power brings the essence of being seen, heard, loved, and embraced. Much like holding a mirror up, reflecting on your Flow of Feelings activates the observer part of your being. It invites you to bear witness to what you are feeling, versus being consumed. This space of bearing witness comes with a nonjudgemental presence for all the feelings that are flowing – when and however they may flow.

There's a story that perfectly demonstrates the power of bearing witness in the midst of Flow of Feelings. We were at a friend's house, and their five-month-old baby was doing well...until suddenly he wasn't. It started with a little whimper that quickly escalated to fully blown tears and red cheeks. His entire little body was clenched, from his hands to his toes. The first attempt at comfort came swiftly from his mom, a human at this point programmed to be on alert as soon as her child cried. Yet, the baby was not soothed by his mom. The next line of cavalry stepped in, yet his dad's typically helpful swinging and shooshing was not productive in alleviating the baby's angst either.

My guy, Patrick, was next in line to offer his best efforts to soothe the kiddo. Before I share what happened, I must offer the caveat that Patrick and I visited for a few hours that evening. We were not living the role of parents to a baby, a toddler, and two teenagers. Our sleep was solid each night and we have kids old enough to communicate their needs and desires. So, Patrick came into this scenario with the advantage of refreshed energy.

The screaming baby was in a vibrating seat at this point. Patrick quietly approached him, seemingly as if nothing was wrong. His approach was soft and quiet. He did not seem eager or urgent about getting the baby to stop crying, rather it felt like he was seeking to understand and simply be with the baby... even amid his distress. Patrick's voice was calm. He lightly touched the baby but not constantly. It was his way of saying, *"Hey, I'm here. You're not alone. Also, though, you're okay."* It came with the sentiment that the baby didn't need anyone to solve this moment for him.

Patrick talked a little bit about the toy on the ground and then interacted with the dog who had come over, curious and seeking some love as well. Mostly though, his energy was calm. It wasn't frantic to solve the situation. It wasn't urgent to understand what was going on. His energy was present. It was allowing and open to the moment that wasn't especially peaceful or joy filled. Patrick just allowed it to be what it was.

Witnessing Patrick in the moment of soothing the crying baby reminded me of what it looks and feels like to bear witness. Even with the most dedicated parents, no amount of breast milk, cradling, patting, or soothing was going to meet his needs. He just needed to let it rip. As a side note for all those parents living through the early weeks and months of child rearing, let's take a moment to acknowledge what a confusing and convoluted process bearing witness can be! You find *yourself* fatigued and potentially in meltdown mode due to lack of proper sleep or food. It's a delicate process of determining whether your fatigue is because of The Interruption – your new family member – or because of poor sleep, movement, and nutrition! The chicken or the egg dilemma does not create ideal space for bearing witness – to yourself or your newborn. As often as possible, slowing ourselves down to decipher between our own grief process and life stressors is crucial. Mostly, kudos! I see you showing up!

What I know is that within about five minutes, the baby calmed down and his tears stopped. It's quite possible he wore himself out. It's also possible he simply needed to get it out. Whatever it was, whatever triggered his otherwise jovial self, he simply needed to get it out.

Obviously, bearing witness to another human can feel like a

tall task! I was on a coaching call discussing the idea of bearing witness with a dear friend and client. As Nan unpacked how much she longed to be witnessed through her role – and grief – of being a care partner to her wife in the late stages of Alzheimer's disease, we quickly identified how rare it is for people to do this for one another. Upon sharing a bit of the heavy part of her Flow of Feelings, Nan said that it is rather common for others to jump in with their own examples of heaviness! Can you imagine – someone opening up and stretching into the power available during Flow of Feelings, only to be met with someone else's weight? Unfortunately, I bet you can imagine...

As our conversation unfolded, in her witty way, Nan said, "*It's like we need to tell people Wipe Your Feet!*" With a chuckle and explanation, she shared bearing witness means NOT filling the space with your own muddy shoes, rather walking gently and being present to the other. Certainly, there's a time and space for mutual rumination, yet in the midst of grief and specifically Flow of Feelings, it's hardly ever the time to bring your own story forward. Another friend's mom says we all need "*emotional raincoats.*" I like this idea melded with the "*wipe your feet*" sentiment, because it helps clarify that things may get messy, yet you are not required to do anything other than simply be available. If it helps to picture yourself putting on an emotional raincoat that serves as a barrier to your energy bubble as well as a reminder to not solve or share – go for it!

While talking about bearing witness, Nan also told me about the Bedouins, a nomadic Arab tribe. She shared how the Bedouins gather under a tent and each person has their own rug to sit on. When it is someone's turn to speak or hold the floor, everyone else rolls their carpet back so they can offer as much space as possible for the person to speak. This allows the one speaking to be front and center and to be the most important in that moment.

Bearing witness may be an ambiguous or foreign concept.

We have not all been raised in the Bedouin culture, or other cultures that have talking sticks. I would suggest a question I sometimes use with family and friends when they are sharing a moment with me. I ask, *"Would you like to be heard, hugged, or helped?"* The answer to this question gets me into the ballpark of what my loved one needs and foregoes my own assumptions or proclivity to race toward solutions. Below are some examples of bearing witness, stemming from these three categories. Ideally, these support your growth toward the power within Flow of Feelings.

When one wants to be **Heard**:
- Actively listen. Some tips for active listening include: make eye contact as the person is sharing, position your body so you can face or lean into the other person, do not interrupt, put your phone down, do not let other distractions take your focus away.
- Ask *"And what else?"* This offers permission for the person to keep sharing.
- Reflect back what you heard the person say. Specifically, focus on and repeat any feelings they may have shared. For example, *"It sounds like this is a really scary and frustrating experience."*
- Send a text or make a call to let the person know you are thinking of them, with the caveat that no response is needed.

When one wants to be **Hugged**:
- Literally hug the person!*
- Hold the person's hand.*
- Place a hand on their shoulder or arm.*
- Wrap your arms around your own torso or shoulders and hug the person energetically.

Please note, it is incredibly important to respect the other's space. If they do not like to be touched, do not. And, even if they don't mind being touched, there are times when touching may seem like the kindest thing to do, yet it interrupts a person's ability to let their feelings flow. So, be clear about whether this is what a person needs at any given moment, versus your own knee jerk reaction to sooth and solve. There is time for all of that, just not necessarily immediately.

When one wants to be **Helped** (I like to say **Supported**):
- Practice curiosity. Ask the person what they *feel* (not what they *think*) would be the next best and loving thing for themselves?
- If you have a suggestion in mind, first ask if they are open to ideas.
- Be ready to act, or enroll support from others, when a direct request is made.

Here's the deal, oftentimes we set up meal and prayer chains, or childcare and assistance with house cleaning. All of this is exceptionally generous. Yet, there are times when there is no casserole needed – just listen! That gem also comes from Nan...she's become infinitely wise through her journey of grief (not to mention her humor has never been more on point!)

Within each Power of Grief, you will notice I share a spectrum. From heavy to neutral to powerful (to be able). If bearing witness feels like too far of a leap to take as you are living or witnessing Flow of Feelings, the neutral option is gentle awareness and curiosity. Nothing radical or drastic is required, rather allow yourself to explore the neutral option. It can feel like the experience of the bit of fresh air wafting through the windows during the early days of spring. As you approach your Flow of Feelings with gentle awareness and curiosity, you begin to dismantle the disdain toward grief, get familiar with simply noticing, shift from your head to your whole being, and finally learn how to create space for yourself to fully absorb the power available for you through your feelings.

I also like the idea that within each Power of Grief is a mini microcosm of all 5 Powers. It harkens Rumi's quote, *"You are not a drop in the ocean. You are the entire ocean in a drop."* Individually, each Power of Grief is unique and essential, like every drop in the ocean. Collectively, The 5 Powers of Grief are interconnected and create the whole, like the entire ocean. In Chapter 10, I offer more visuals to help solidify this concept.

Ultimately, can you feel depressed and still know you are ok? Yes. Can you feel scared and also choose to not run? Yes. Can you lay down some of your responsibilities to ensure you are resting, eating, and moving in the midst of your Flow of Feelings? Yes. Harder, I realize – believe me, I live and battle this too often on a daily basis. Yet, I've come to realize that people are open to being gentle with me and picking up some slack, or giving plenty of grace, when I let them know that is what I need. What I once considered adding undue burden to others by speaking forward what I needed in the midst of grieving has now become the pathway forward. Inviting myself and others to bear witness to my Flow of Feelings has literally moved me one step closer to alchemizing grief.

I ascribe to both the K.I.S.S. (Keep it Simple Silly) philosophy and Robert Fulghum's idea of *All I Really Needed to Know I Learned in Kindergarten*. So, as we practice gentle awareness, curiosity, and bearing witness to our feelings, I want to share an emotion wheel. The emotion wheel was first developed by Robert Plutchik, an American psychologist who researched the study of emotions, among other topics.

The concept behind the wheel is that humans often boil our emotions down to six primal feelings: Happy, Surprised, Peaceful, Sad, Anger, Fear. From there, additionally complex emotions that stem from each of these six basic feelings are offered in two additional rings. The goal is to increase self-awareness, grow emotional regulation, learn how to communicate our emotions, and use it as a tool for understanding others.

Take a moment and explore the emotions wheel.

Are there emotions you've never felt?
Are there feelings you've never dared to articulate?
Do you find you predominantly live in a specific wedge?
Does any wedge create comfort or anxiousness within you?

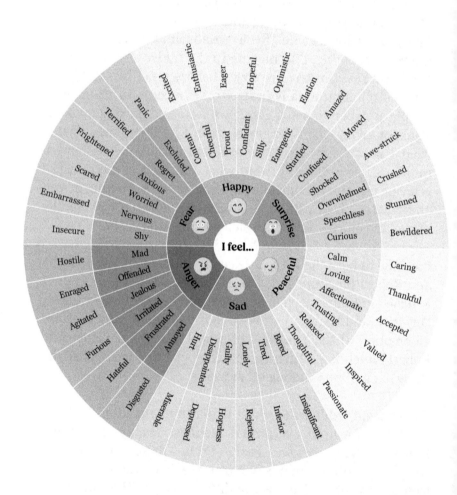

I printed this wheel and put it on the side of my refrigerator. It serves as a reminder for the two adults and two teens in our household. We are complex beings, and it is important for us to experience the whole spectrum of emotions. Even with this daily reminder posted in my home, I have lived far too many moments of neglecting my wedge of sadness. And heaven forbid I tap into my feelings of anger! This joyful and blessed spirit...how could I be angry about anything? I believe this is what some have come to call toxic positivity. Even though I have always held space for others' wide range of emotions, I historically limited myself.

I used to equate emotional intelligence with not being angry. Go ahead and giggle, because we know emotional intelligence is actually the ability to manage your own emotions including the full range and understand the emotions of those around you. It integrates self-awareness with self-regulation, motivation, empathy, and social skills. And, believe it or not, empathy can and must be turned in and shared with ourselves as well!

The way I see it, I avoided the anger wedge to a fault for many years. I did not let myself go there...which does not stop the feeling, rather it stops it up! It was as if I was giving a big middle finger to myself anytime an ounce of annoyance, frustration, jealousy, or disgust crept up. I developed a skill of pivoting to some variation of surprise or peace to keep any anger from rearing its head. All these years later, I finally see that it is okay to feel these feelings. It's taken a while to untrain my brain to avoid what is unfamiliar, yet here I am – a reformed human. Now, when I feel angry, I can name it for myself and be responsible in how I engage with others. Just like when I feel happy.

I heard this too during an interview about the grief involved when getting fired. The person shared that the initial gut punch to his ego was quickly followed by feeling stupid, beating himself up, and then feeling a bit victim-y. Yet, as he allowed the feelings to flow, they were less consuming and he was able to reflect and ask himself, *"Okay, how did I contribute to this?"* This is gentle awareness and curiosity in action. He was then able to expand from fear, anger, and sadness to a much wider array of emotions.

Self-awareness is important. I was reminded by an expert clinical social worker that we can't necessarily control what feelings sweep through us in any given moment, but a thought is just a thought, and a feeling is just a feeling. It doesn't make it an action. It doesn't make it a reality.

The Emotion Wheel is a tool we can use in everyday life to grow our self-awareness. Whether you throw a dart or simply pick an emotion to explore, it is worth diversifying your emotional bandwidth in moments when you have more available – you know, when you're not actively grieving! Then, when grief strikes, you'll be familiar and better equipped to practice the power of Flow of Feelings – bearing witness to yourself and others.

In Chapter Seven, I will dive into the delineation between Flow of Feelings and Breaking – the fourth Power of Grief, as these can be somewhat difficult to discern at times.

6

Holding

Holding: This is when we cling to the past: dreams, relationships, routines, and life before The Interruption.

Have you ever caught yourself holding your breath?

When you jump in a pool or lake, you hold your breath while you go underwater. When you come to the surface again, you release that hold and refill your lungs.

You may involuntarily hold your breath when you are startled or afraid. Your exhale comes when the moment or danger has dissipated.

What about when you are bracing for what's ahead, maybe as you plummet down the steep slope of a roller coaster or instinctively grab the *"Oh shit!"* handle in the car when someone else is driving and you have zero control. Have you ever clutched the steering wheel with white knuckles while driving through a stressful environment?

Holding.
  Bracing.
    Clinging on while we get through something.

Time and time again, I notice in the midst of grief – when an interruption happens, and my feelings are flowing – the next part of my process is Holding. The heavy perspective of Holding is having a backward facing focus.

As I interviewed people, three common themes surfaced: 1) the notion of holding onto guilt and regret for things not said or done while there was still time; 2) shame over things that could not be changed; and 3) selfish desires that things would be different. This is where the interwovenness of The 5 Powers of Grief is so noticeable. The feelings of guilt, regret, and shame all cause a person to hold on to something that once was. To uncover and differentiate Flow of Feelings from Holding, one of the questions I ask in relation to a specific interruption is, *"What has been the hardest to let go of?"* This question calls forward what a person has been holding throughout their grief.

I want to take a moment to clarify one of the things that came up in many interviews and conversations: Feeling selfish. Whether it was the desire to be present when a loved one took their last breath, the sadness of no longer having your best friend to talk to because they are living with dementia, or the mom who loves her newborn though equally misses the identity she once knew to be herself – feeling selfish is actually a reflection of self-care. Our society has twisted it all up, in my opinion. There is a clear delineation between *feeling* selfish and *being* selfish! Your feelings are just that – feelings. They do not define you! However, even *being* selfish does not mean you are bad...especially when you are living through an experience of grief! Being selfish enables you to reflect and get clear about what makes you feel safe and what you are longing for – and often offers guidance on how to grow from one to the other. Even if it surfaces abruptly or demands attention, selfishness can be a beautiful awareness moment. If nothing else, please know that while you are grieving, the feeling of selfishness may have a wise message to deliver to you. It may unlock the heaviness and move you into the Powers of Grief...if you give yourself permission to be curious and learn from it.

Soap box moment complete. Back to our conversation about the third Power of Grief: Holding.

When I was diagnosed with breast cancer, it felt like life spun out of control. I had multiple health care providers calling, scheduling appointments, and walking me through the steps that were about to happen. I had a fast-growing type of cancer, so it was important for us to take action quickly. Within three weeks of the diagnosis, I had my first surgery to place the port. Two weeks later, I was hooked up to machines and being pumped full of two types of chemotherapy, two types of targeted therapy, and additional supplements and fluids to assist my body through it all.

It's easy to tap into the Flow of Feelings, even now. I was angry and scared. I felt completely out of control and just as soon as one appointment was scheduled, something else would get changed. I was panicked about my business and my income. As an entrepreneur, just three and a half years into my coaching and leadership development business, I had finally secured several lucrative contracts and a base of clients. So, amid the most gnarly interruption of my life, I held onto what I could. I looked at the calendar and marked the days I would likely be able to work, based on typical side effects the medical professionals anticipated. I talked to contract leads to wrap up what I could and negotiated how to be present for the ongoing projects.

And...I continued to panic. As strong as my hold to my previous plan was, so too was the awareness that it was not going to work. Which only sent me into a deeper, heavier Flow of Feelings.

No one faulted me for holding on to my life before the diagnosis. It was what I knew, and it was what felt safe. To me, it was seemingly necessary. Everyone allowed me to have my process. This truth was likely my first entrée to the fourth Power of Grief – Breaking. We'll get to that in good time though...I promise.

To state the obvious, we're not very versed in letting go. It happens all the time, yet it is often more of a tugging and ripping versus gentle parting. Which is why I needed to put words to the neutral and powerful vantage point of Holding to help me shift out of what felt so heavy. I realized at the other end of the spectrum, the power in Holding, is being present. Simple enough, right? Of course, in the midst of a cancer diagnosis, a divorce, the loss of a job, or the death of a loved one it is not simple at all. The tug to look back at what was is compelling. Yet, the call to be where our feet are...to be truly present...*that* is when we begin to recognize that Holding has different versions available.

Imagine holding a baby chick in your hand. If you are a toddler, holding that chick likely involves wrapping your fingers around it and squeezing just a bit too hard. It's too tight of a hold on something that needs space to move and breath and be. If you are an adult, holding that chick probably involves an open palm, ever so slightly cupped to create a mini cradle of support for the chick. Both are holding – one is a better option for the chick!

That simple image of "open hand holding" the chick allows me to see there is more than one way of approaching the task. It's almost comical – as adults, we would scurry in to assist the child in this scenario to be gentle with the chick and to release their grip. Yet, when life happens to us, we hold on tight, don't we? There's instinct and longing involved.

Shifting into the power of Holding is challenging, or at least it was for me throughout the journey of healing with and through breast cancer. Every time I practiced being present, I would either experience a tidal wave of feelings or something else would be thrown into the mix that I did not expect...sending me straight back into the heaviness of Holding again.

My friend, Lindsey, who is witnessing her second of four children graduate from high school, has been vocal about how challenging this milestone and transition has been – mentally, physically, emotionally. She's not doing great. When I asked her what was different about this graduation as compared to her oldest finishing high school, her response was telling. Lindsey shared, "*When Evie graduated, I was focused on checking all the boxes - making sure all the tasks were complete. I was in my head. This time around, I am much more in my heart, which is why I am feeling so much more!"*

Interesting perspective, isn't it? Lindsey's experience is similar to when a loved one dies and there are details to tend to: taking care of the body, ending any care services, getting the news out to family and friends, writing an obituary, meeting with the funeral home, choosing details for a service, choosing the outfit your loved one will be laid to rest in or if they will be cremated, choosing a casket or urn, scheduling the service, inviting people to pay their respects, coordinating food and accommodations for guests, addressing final bills, closing accounts, submitting paperwork for a death certificate, waiting for the official death certificate to arrive to finalize closing accounts...and on and on. With so many things to DO there is little to no bandwidth to BE or FEEL. Yet, the feelings are right there...under the surface, begging to be tended to. Still though – we hold. We hold onto the tangible tasks to keep us moving...one foot in front of the other. We hold onto the belief that we must be strong, or that the tasks are more urgent than our own grieving process.

I believe it's important to bring a gentle awareness to how we often approach an interruption of any kind, and a curiosity if this way is serving us well? Gentle awareness and curiosity – the neutral position within Holding. By now, you are likely sensing the theme that gentle awareness and curiosity are the neutral position for all 5 Powers of Grief. Because the truth is, sometimes it's too far of a stretch to move from the heaviness to the power. In those moments, it is necessary to have a smaller step option. A subtle move that allows us to feel less heavy is important when we are not yet ready to be powerful.

I lived in gentle awareness quite a bit throughout the early months of breast cancer. These moments would come in the form of sitting still after a phone call from a medical provider or laying on the couch taking deep breaths – literally guiding myself to fill my lungs and belly and then let all the air out.

Over and over again. It felt like I was living in the twilight zone. I did not feel present. I did not know which way was up. I felt lost, yet I was just letting that be. Gentle awareness and curiosity melted away my self judgement. It honored whatever space I found myself in. It allowed for the fog, the momentum, the resting, the wide-awake nights – it simply allows.

And at some point, you get present. That may mean more feelings rush in, like Lindsey in the midst of her second child graduating from high school. It may mean you make different choices or stay the course. Whatever surfaces during your presence in Holding is important. Because *you* are important and *your process* is important. When you find your way to open hand holding, you have unlocked the power of this phase of grief.

7

Breaking

Breaking: Finally, from either internal or external pressure, we break our hold of what was. Breaking can seem scary, yet it is necessary in our process. Breaking allows space for the new.

The first three Powers of Grief happen without much or any effort. An interruption occurs – a diagnosis, a car accident, a project shift or layoff at work, a broken bone, a death. The Flow of Feelings rush in, responsive to said interruption – frustration, shock, fear, anger, disappointment, discomfort, and sometimes even joy and excitement. And very easily, we slide into Holding, giving our best effort to keep everything together, striving to keep the pace and direction we were headed before The Interruption happened. Essentially looking back at what was and clinging...holding in an attempt to have that back again.

The fourth and fifth Powers of Grief require greater intentionality, in my experience. Because of this, I suspect these two Powers of Grief are not tapped into as often or as deeply, thus leaving us in a cycle of the first three Powers that can seem endless and heavy.

My expert move in moments that seem too complicated for me to figure out on my own is to seek wisdom from nature. The Academy of Natural Sciences of Drexel University offers a clear understanding of the development of most butterflies. While there are always outliers like moths and unique species, butterflies typically have a three to four-week lifespan from egg to adult and death. From a pinhead-sized egg, the larva's job is to eat. During this phase, which can last from a few days to a couple weeks, the larva can grow 100 times their original size. The larva literally splits and sheds four to five times as it grows.

Let that sink in for a moment. Larva split and shed in order to grow! It sounds a bit painful, yet also pretty awe-inspiring. This is the journey they are on to become everything they were meant to be. It is their natural progression that they do not resist.

Once fully grown, and now commonly referred to as a caterpillar, they take the next monumental step in their process. The caterpillar transforms into a pupa, also known as a chrysalis. During this one to two-week process (some species take up to two years in the chrysalis phase), special cells present in the larva now begin to grow rapidly. The transition from a caterpillar with a few tiny eyes, stubby legs, and very short antennae takes place. Within the chrysalis these parts grow into long legs, long antennae, compound eyes, and colorful wings.

The butterfly emerges from the chrysalis, taking some time for its wings to open and ultimately fly. Now its job is to lay eggs to once again begin the cycle. Most adult butterflies live one to two weeks.

What strikes me about this process that is often referenced in relation to growing and evolving is the percentage of time spent in the phase of the chrysalis – the death and transformation of the caterpillar to the butterfly. This phase represents 30-50% of the creature's whole life...which feels like a big deal to note! Yet to the butterfly it is just part of the whole journey.

To be clear, I am not wishing 30-50% of our lives to be spent in the Fourth Power of Grief – Breaking. I am, however, intrigued that nature may alert us to the fact that death of oneself is far more prominent and important than we humans, especially within our American culture, like to acknowledge.

Part of my message is to say, *"Don't settle."* Don't be a smaller version of yourself! We must all continue to molt and evolve, to grow and recenter so we are ready for whatever is next in our wild and precious lives!

When interviewing my partner Patrick about his experience through the grief of being fired and laid off, he offered some wisdom that feels relevant here.

"I once listened to an interview with John Belushi. When his brother died, it was a very poignant time for him that caused a lot of grief and anger. John went to South America and did an Ayahuasca retreat. At the retreat, there was a shaman guide who reflected to John that he was no longer in control of his brain. He said he had released control to anger and anger was now at the head of the conference table, directing how the meeting went. The shaman told John that he had the power to kick anger out of that chair — to tell him to go back to his own chair — and to take the meeting back over."

Patrick went on to say, *"When you're sitting in your conference room (life), Grief will knock on the door. It will poke its little head in, like, "Hey buddy" and then all those other things just barrel through. Anger, sadness, resentment, shame all rush in, meanwhile they push grief into the room. They're yelling and screaming all sorts of unkind messages. All these other feelings are running the meeting, but grief is just kind of sitting in the corner. It's the one who knocked on the door, which is why it gets such a bad wrap, but it's all these other emotions that don't make you feel good. Grief doesn't make you feel good, but it is the thing that gives you the space to heal.*

In my experience, when I got the other voices to quiet down, I was able to say, "That job wasn't a good fit. And, I don't have to work with that person now." In that moment, there was a crack of light that broke through and allowed me to realize and accept it was ok not to have that job anymore. Whatever your grief may be, it's when you have that crack and the light comes in...that's when the ugly voices shut up. That's when grief finally has a chance to speak. Most often it says, "That sucked. What are you going to do with it now?" Grief is growth. The other stuff is the weed killer. It pummels you with statements and accusations. Grief lets you name that it sucked, recognizes your resilience, and asks you to look for what's possible now."

In Japanese culture, *Kintsugi* is an art practice and philosophy that encourages viewing broken objects as valuable and meaningful, versus discarding them. In this form of art, broken ceramic pieces are fused back together using *urushi* lacquer and gold, which emphasize the piece's cracks and breaks. In *Kintsugi*, which means "golden joinery", the flaws are celebrated as the most valuable part of the piece, which is also a metaphor for embracing imperfection and resilience in life.

This art form harkens a lesson my dad taught me when I was younger and aspiring to be as talented as my sister in art endeavors. Of course, both my parents taught me to be my own unique self, yet having a sister talented in so many ways often served as a beacon and path for me. I wanted to be like her and do the things she did. I would inevitably end up with very different projects than Patrice – either in the category of "Pinterest fail" or something completely unique in its own right. Even in the midst of my early developmental years, dad would teach the Navajo's lesson. This tribe believed that nothing was perfect, except for the Gods, so in anything they created, they included a deliberate imperfection. This was to honor that in the pursuit of harmony and balance, we live deeply imperfect lives...and that is ok! I remember the thick resistance I felt early on when I was taught this wise practice. Yet over time, I have embraced the tradition and now more readily celebrate the parts of projects that are less than perfect.

Finding beauty in the imperfect, incomplete, and simple... what a radical way of viewing all the little and big moments of life! Yet again, the Japanese have a word for this: *wabi-sabi*. Closely related to the philosophy of *Kintsugi*, *wabi-sabi* is a belief that stretches beyond simply embracing imperfections, it is a way of life in which beauty is found in oneself and others, even in the midst of imperfections.

I actually feel my muscles relaxing and a calmness flowing through me as I write about these philosophies of life embodied in other cultures. It does not escape me how restrictive and therefore brittle, and at times fragile, my own mental stories have made me in moments of life. And while I'm willing to be responsible for myself and my beliefs, there's also something to note here about our cultural norms. When we look outside the culture that has been glorified within largely Caucasian, middle- and upper-class communities in the United States, it's easy to find joy in simplicity, flow in relationships, and ease in basic humanity.

The contrasting feelings of rigidity and self-righteousness – both of which I have lived many times in my life – are so constricting and entirely deflating. This leads me to discuss our resistance to breaking. Or, at least the resistance I have felt throughout my life as I've attempted to "hold it all together" and "not drop any juggling balls". I don't want others to be able to relate, yet in all the conversations I've had, breaking brings a feeling of yuck and displeasure. I assure you, you are not alone in this feeling...and this is why I want to spend some time on the notion of breaking.

As I ponder the language we use, I see the term 'break' show up in undesirable ways:

Break up
Break down
Break your heart
Break your spirit
Break the rules/the law

I find it interesting to notice though that there are some neutral uses of the word within our vernacular as well, such as daybreak, breakfast, breaking news, and break dance. I throw that last one in with a giggle, and awareness that the word break is used in so many forms, both as a verb and a noun. There are even positive experiences of breaking:

Break through
Break a Leg
Lunch break
Break a habit
Break a fall

All of this to say, our language is complex yet time and time again, hesitance is the feeling so easily embodied when we speak about breaking. The following image found its way to me several years back and expanded my understanding of breaking in a very tangible way.

If an egg is broken
by outside force,
life ends.

If broken by
inside force,
life begins.

Great things always
begin from the inside.

–Jim Kwik, Brain Coach & Author

This picture and message made an impact on me and allowed me to grapple with the concept that breaking is inevitable. How and why I break is the deeper question. Is my breaking from external pressure – expectations, judgement, or pace – or from internal pressure – growth and resilience? Either way, I am destined to break...so why fight that truth?

Pause for a moment and marinate in this idea. What emerges when you focus on the notion: *I am going to break time and time again in life. Will my breaking be from external pressure or internal pressure?*

Think of it this way, can you recall a time at work or home when you were nose to the grindstone, working on something that had a definitive deadline? You felt stressed, when suddenly someone cracked a joke. For a moment, you looked up and laughed. You broke the tension. Or they did. Either way, it was a breaking moment. There is power in breaking.

There is another Japanese word I find intriguing in light of the fourth Power of Grief: *misogi*. This is a purification ritual rooted in Shinto tradition. The purpose of *misogi* is to purify the body and spirit. It represents spiritual cleansing and reconnection with nature and the divine. Although *misogi* is typically done by standing under the cold water of a waterfall or immersion in cold water, it points to the notion of transformation. The goal is to create personal growth and resilience by facing personal fears, doubts and weaknesses. The power within Breaking is resilience. I am not telling you to do a cold-water plunge (although there is ample research outlining the health benefits of this practice), rather sharing more wisdom we can glean from other cultures. As we evolve our own cultural norms, perhaps breaking can be viewed as an act of growth and resilience.

As you ease into and extend to others this idea that breaking is inevitable, there is permission granted for each of us to be in harmony with the ebb and flow of life...to have realistic expectations...to not hold ourselves to unrealistic standards. There's that word again – hold – in relation to standards that are not realistic. Holding has a time and a purpose, as does breaking.

Breaking, the fourth Power of Grief, very purposefully follows Holding. When we are holding, it is difficult to see the whole picture. Our lens is narrow, dark, and rigid. As we release our hold to what was, we break. Through the cracks that are formed, light can shine through. Light that offers clarity and understanding that was not available in the midst of holding so tightly to what was. The light represents and offers space for something new to appear.

In breaking there are cracks,

 with cracks there is light,

  with light we can see a greater picture and,

   we come to know ourselves as resilient.

After many rounds of living and observing The 5 Powers of Grief, I have noticed that with a snap of the fingers, each of us experiences The Interruption, Flow of Feelings, and Holding, time and time again. These first three powers simply happen. Even if we instigate The Interruption, it occurs and sets off a chain reaction that empowers Flow of Feelings and Holding to quickly activate as well.

Breaking, however, requires intentionality. A friend spoke a profound truth as she was reflecting in the midst of her divorce, "*Breaking can feel so isolating.*" This is an example of Flow of Feelings and Breaking becoming intertwined. It happens all the time and feels confusing. Yet, one way I have found to navigate this is to ask myself a few questions. Since I often start with what I *think*, I don't have to intentionally ask myself that question very often. It is important to ask yourself: "*What do I think?*" in order to set up the second self-reflection question: *How do I feel?* This is an invitation to be more than a brain on a stick walking around! This question offers curiosity and permission to reflect inward. When I am curious about what I think *and* how I feel, there is greater opportunity for clarity to arrive. And, it allows me to be honest about what I need at any given moment. I sense as we explore the notion of breaking, this is a great way to remain rooted in ourselves and our personal power – because it can seem rather unnerving!

The Power of Breaking is where I believe David Kessler's wisdom *"Grief demands a witness"* comes into play. Whether or not we anticipate grief, it is possible for us to live through the first three Powers without being witnessed by another, and at times even by ourselves. As humans, we are skilled at masking, avoiding, and diverting attention from undesirable things. Personally, and communally, our culture has often categorized The Interruption and Flow of Feelings as undesirable. Holding is a bit more neutral, in my experience, because it's understandable. We want to hold onto what was. We want to remain in our comfort zone.

Breaking is known to be messy. And being messy is not historically desirable. Through my divorce, job transitions, thyroid and breast cancer, and a number of other interruptions in life, I was afraid breaking would be burdensome to others. I did not want to create a mess that rippled out and impacted anyone else. So, I held "it" together.

Yet, in breaking I was able to breathe again.
I no longer held my breath.

The intentionality of breaking is nuanced and simple, all at once. As with grieving in general, there is no right or wrong way and there is certainly no roadmap. Yet, as I've socialized these concepts, I have been asked many times, *"So, how do I break?"* With some reflection, I believe the secret lies in a dual faceted answer. Asking for *and* receiving support.

This is where Patrick would say, *"Ewww!"* After several years together, and this standard response, we laugh and proceed... knowing that we get to practice asking for and receiving support each and every day.

Getting more specific with what I've gleaned, I have come to realize that if a person identifies as an introvert, their breaking will likely require reaching out and requesting support and witnessing from others. Transversely, if a person identifies as being an extrovert, their breaking will likely require reaching in and being witnessed by self.

Don't get me wrong, I believe being witnessed by self *and* others is necessary for a rich and full experience with grief. Yet, I have noticed when we live in the swirl of the first three Powers, it's easy to default to our most safe and comfortable default mechanisms. These safe and easy ways are important, though they will not take us all the way. Which is why swinging the pendulum from our default ways to the other extreme is likely what will create a break within us – ensuring the pressure of the break comes from within...representing growth and life.

As we delve into the notion of breaking, I wanted to share a few stories to serve as examples.

My breast cancer diagnosis came when I was 45 years old. It was the fourth year of my coaching and leadership development business, and I was finally hitting a cadence that facilitated the fun and funds I craved.

Then, breast cancer – The Interruption.

As shared earlier, I lived in Holding for four to six weeks before I acknowledged I was losing hold of the life I was desperately clinging to – my business, my relationships, my abundant life. All of it felt like it was slipping through my fingers. My phone dinged routinely as new appointments were added to MyChart and procedures scheduled. My calendar was no longer mine, and it became clear between treatments, procedures, follow up appointments, and side effects of the chemotherapy, I was not going to be able to keep my business alive while also walking this journey.

One of my first breaks happened after a dear friend asked, "*What do you need?*" Candace is direct and supportive, fierce and loving in how she shows up for me and others. Her question was not asked from the typical chaos that revolves around any sort of medical issue, rather far more direct. She was asking what I needed financially...talk about unnerving! I had the option to tighten my grip on a bank account void of a hefty reserve with months of treatments and surgeries looming along with five-digit deductibles spanning two years or break my silence...my pride...my stress.

I recall sitting down and drafting a document that outlined my need:

√ $35,000 for medical deductibles over two years (yes, disgustingly high and addressed once I got through this hurdle)

√ $25,000 to pay my mortgage and bills for the 10 months of no income I anticipated

Sixty thousand dollars. I needed $60,000.

It nearly turns my stomach again as I write it now. I sobbed at this number. I was sickened by my astronomical annual deductible that I secured through market place insurance when I went out on my own in 2020. My monthly expenses were whittled down to the smallest possible number to account for my mortgage, monthly utilities, and groceries yet this added up to SUCH a big number! Having to say this out loud to Patrick, my parents, and Candace – it was a breaking moment. It was the breaking of the stereotypical secrecy of shrouded finances. Breaking of my radical independence. Mostly, breaking my, *"I'll figure this out myself"* mentality.

It was terrifying to say the number out loud and equally perplexing to understand what would happen next. The heavy side of Breaking is the lack of clarity of what else is possible, and I was living in that heaviness. I legitimately had no idea what to do as I numbly went from appointment to appointment, with a growing understanding of the magnitude of what was ahead. But let me tell you what happened next.

I said the number. Candace, equal parts nonchalant and passion, said *"Ok, I've got you. We're going to call on your circle of support and fundraise sixty thousand dollars to get you through this. Done."* Just like that, as she took the weight of finances off me, my entire being shattered. Although I felt incredibly humbled to know such a big ask was about to be cast into the world on my behalf, I was relieved to release the hold on one pretty crushing, external weight.

Within ninety days, Candace had spearheaded raising sixty-thousand dollars. She did this for my well-being in the midst of dis-ease. Hundreds of family members, friends from long ago and recent days, past colleagues, and friends of friends and family donated. Ten dollars to six thousand dollars, the amounts varied and added up. I also spent the few ounces of energy I had early on submitting financial aid applications to various nonprofits, inquiring about eligibility for aid through the pharmaceutical companies who manufactured the poison being pumped into me, and petitioning the hospital's financial aid office. All of this added up to the dollars I needed to get me through my journey that ended up spanning a total of seventeen months.

I could not have survived without breaking open to the tremendous outpouring of love and support from people near and far. I equally could not have ever imagined making such a big ask to be supported. I remember crumbling to tears as mail arrived with a note and $100 check, or a grocery gift card, or $1,000 of cash handed to me. I needed to break in order for the love and support to seep in through the cracks.

Throughout the journey, my parents traveled the two hundred mile, one way trip every three weeks and they spent several days with me after each chemo treatment. Together, we learned the cadence of when I would need to return to the hospital for extra fluids and additional shots. We knew when I would be in a dark hole of fatigue, aches, and sickness. My parents made sure to be there during those dark days – quietly cleaning my house, making meals that I ate very little of, and being present however I needed in my waking moments. Together, we got through chemo and proceeded to the next step of the process – my double mastectomy and ongoing targeted therapy infusions. After that, came my reconstruction surgery.

I opted for DIEP Flap reconstruction. This is an intensive surgery created in the late 1980's and used since the mid 90's for breast reconstruction. A football shaped flap of skin and tissue is dissected from the abdomen and used to reconstruct breasts. This meant my breasts would be my own tissue. It also meant a 10-hour surgery, which turned into 13 hours as the skilled surgeon relocated and connected tiny blood vessels to fuel the tissue in an entirely different part of my body.

When I was educated on the details of this surgery, I was devastated to learn that they would remove my belly button – the part of me that originally connected me to my mom. Fortunately, my exceptional surgeon was able to transplant my belly button. Yes, you read that right! My original belly button was transplanted to my midriff, and after many months of scabbing is alive and well.

All of this to say, my reconstruction surgery was intense. It required four days and nights in the ICU Burn Unit, due to skin grafting. It required three weeks of walking hunched over in order to allow adequate healing for my body. It required a couple months of sleeping in a lift recliner to assist my muscles that had been maneuvered around.

After returning home from my reconstruction surgery, mom and dad once again moved in to care for me for three weeks this time. They uprooted their lives to care for their adult child. Which led to another breaking moment for me.

Every few days, I would garner enough energy (though decently devoid of desire) to shower. It was a two-person ordeal, my role mainly getting in and out of the shower and holding the four drains that protruded from my chest and hips. Mom's role was to reach in and wash my half inch locks of hair, scrub my back, and delicately run the soapy cloth under my newly built breasts. She would carefully dry me from head to toe after each shower and tend to the dressings that helped keep my drains as minimally irritated as possible.

If you have never been bathed by another as an adult, I can tell you it is one of the most intimate and vulnerable things you may ever do. For me, it harkened my Catholic upbringing of Jesus washing the feet of those he loved. My mom, well into seven decades of life, went the distance to serve me in the most tangible way possible. She made me feel safe and loved. She was care-filled and went as fast or as slow as I needed. For me, it was the ultimate act of surrender to sit naked on the shower bench and be bathed.

Breaking. Breaking free from the past belief I held around what it meant to be an adult and care for myself. Breaking open to such gentle, loving care from my mom who would do anything for me. Perhaps by this point in my journey of healing with and through breast cancer I was fairly versed at asking for and receiving support, because breaking into a thousand pieces in this instance felt like coming home. It was delicate and deliberate. Finally, I did not fight the break...rather I knew it was for me, and it did not represent the end.

A couple other breakings I vividly recall were seated in chairs. One was with my counselor and the other with a hair dresser.

My counselor through Cancer Family Care based in Cincinnati, Ohio was a kind and steady presence of listening and support during the times I was able to garner the energy to see him. During one visit in the early months of 2025, the year I deemed as my Build Year: Building energy, stamina, mental clarity, emotional regulation, and more – I said to Paul, *"I want to acknowledge myself for where I am and how well I'm doing."* As soon as I said those words I felt the familiar tightening on the grip of humility and outward versus inward focus. Yet, Paul's kind face invited me to go for it. I rattled off what I felt proud of myself for: My daily yoga stretches, my return to part time work, my excitement for the next step in my relationship with Patrick and the kids, my forward focus. It was quite a list. As I said it out loud and invited Paul to witness me, I felt myself shining like I had not in a very long time. I felt alive and well, that break felt good. Proud and able. It was a breaking of past ways and letting someone else witness me.

The other moment happened sitting in a salon, nearly twenty months after my hair began falling out in clumps from chemotherapy. I had gotten the hairs on the nap of my neck and around my ears trimmed once or twice at home but had not yet returned to a salon and paid for the care and detail that come with the whole experience! I was excited to be at this point of hair regrowth, though I did not see the break coming. As I sat in the chair, tilted back to have my hair washed, tears rolled from the sides of my eyes down both sides of my face. I can still feel it now. Again, it was the surrender – the allowing another to minister to me in such an intimate and loving way. I had been showering and washing my steadily growing locks for months at this point, impatient with how the curls did not seem to grow quickly. Yet, having my hair washed for me... Wow! I was literally shattered open to receive.

This is the power of breaking. It is both witnessing ourselves *and* allowing others to witness us in the midst of grief. It is the yin and yang that create the whole. Without both, we do not allow for the full experience of grief – which includes moving within and through us. Grief is not meant to sit in one place forever...and it surely does not. It seeks to seep out of the cracks, much like water finds its way through cracks and crevices. Grief is fluid and must be witnessed in a whole and holy way.

Three weeks after interviewing my friend Elizabeth about her grief journeys, we were together again. Elizabeth's eyes welled with tears as she told me, "*Within a day of talking to you, my body seemed to come back online. It's not back 100% yet, but something changed for the better.*" I reflected to her with a deep knowing as well as abundant awe, "*You let yourself be heard and witnessed. You broke your hold on what was so hard and heavy in your life right now.*" We gripped each other in a hug, with tears of gratitude rolling down our cheeks.

Breaking happens when we ask for support. It also often happens when we're tired of holding. Another way to say that is: Breaking happens at the point of surrender. When we think we can't do it any longer and we finally open to what else can be. Once we break, it can either quickly roll into the Power of Re-Membering – like making scrambled eggs from the broken egg versus slowing and carefully separating the yolk. Or breaking can take longer to garner the gifts from the experience.

The more often I name that I am in a moment or season of Breaking, the less time I need to stay in this space. Much like practicing a sport or musical instrument, the more you do it the less time it requires to hit the note or land the shot when you want to play. As I choose breaking, I lean into the power available: resilience.

My work alongside humans living with Alzheimer's or other forms of dementia and their care partners has pointed me to a powerful poem titled *Welcome To Holland* by Emily Perl Kingsley. This was again shared during the interview with Elizabeth, as she relayed her journey through grief of a child possibly being diagnosed with autism spectrum disorder (ASD). Kingsley's passage was written during her own experience of raising a child with a disability. It rocks me every time I read or hear it, and it strikes me as a beautiful segway from Breaking to Re-Membering.

Welcome to Holland

I am often asked to describe the experience of raising a child with a disability - to try to help people who have not shared that unique experience to understand it, to imagine how it would feel. It's like this......

When you're going to have a baby, it's like planning a fabulous vacation trip - to Italy. You buy a bunch of guide books and make your wonderful plans. The Coliseum. The Michelangelo David. The gondolas in Venice. You may learn some handy phrases in Italian. It's all very exciting.

After months of eager anticipation, the day finally arrives. You pack your bags and off you go. Several hours later, the plane lands. The flight attendant comes in and says, "Welcome to Holland."

"Holland?!?" you say. "What do you mean Holland?? I signed up for Italy! I'm supposed to be in Italy. All my life I've dreamed of going to Italy."

But there's been a change in the flight plan. They've landed in Holland and there you must stay.

The important thing is that they haven't taken you to a horrible, disgusting, filthy place, full of pestilence, famine and disease. It's just a different place.

So you must go out and buy new guide books. And you must learn a whole new language. And you will meet a whole new group of people you would never have met.

It's just a different place. It's slower-paced than Italy, less flashy than Italy. But after you've been there for a while and you catch your breath, you look around.... and you begin to notice that Holland has windmills....and Holland has tulips. Holland even has Rembrandts.

But everyone you know is busy coming and going from Italy... and they're all bragging about what a wonderful time they had there. And for the rest of your life, you will say "Yes, that's where I was supposed to go. That's what I had planned."

And the pain of that will never, ever, ever, ever go away... because the loss of that dream is a very very significant loss.

But... if you spend your life mourning the fact that you didn't get to Italy, you may never be free to enjoy the very special, the very lovely things ... about Holland.

By Emily Perl Kingsley

8

Re-Membering

Re-Membering: With space for the new, we begin to rebuild by weaving together the past, present, and future into a refreshed tapestry. It honors what has been and creates a path forward.

So, here you are.

Holland...

A foreign place you never expected to visit.

What now?

As you begin to digest this new place, you look around and notice. You're curious and perhaps even surprised to sense some peace, gratitude, compassion, and joy within yourself.

Stepping into the fifth Power of Grief, I'd like to take a moment to revisit the root of the word power. Power comes from the Latin root, meaning *"to be able."*

To be able.

Feel that. It is full of possibilities and trust.

There's resiliency – the power within Breaking. Perhaps there is some faith and hope.

To be able in any moment of life means there is an opportunity to create something new.

Once we find ourselves in the Power of Breaking, we begin to realize it is not the end, rather a step in a process that is important and necessary. Much like a baseball player must touch all four bases to have a successful home run, we must also ensure we touch all 5 Powers of Grief for it to be complete, whole, and full of power in our lives. Neglecting to touch any one of the five creates a void that catches us in a never-ending loop of grief. As in life, if you skip a stage of development, you will have to pause, go back, and do that stage before you can move on.

Anytime we find the prefix "re" it means "back" or "again". For the purpose of this Power, I focus on the "again" factor of "re". In my experience, grief can catapult us into feeling consumed, looking back at what was, being unclear and unsure that there's a future, and getting messy. Messiness is the heavy side of Re-Membering. The power is being creative. Within each power of grief, we are asked to touch both ends of the spectrum in order to deeply activate the power that is available. If we never feel messy, we may not be inspired, curious, or creative in finding a new way forward.

I picture Re-Membering like creating a mosaic. Whatever has broken into a thousand beautiful and jagged pieces in the process of Breaking is in front of you. During Re-Membering, you take some pieces from your past, some pieces from the present, and some pieces of what you hope for your future.

Re-Membering happens individually and communally. If you were alive during 9/11, you likely recall that tragic interruption – down to your exact location when the planes hit the World Trade Center towers. As a country, we experienced deep grief including a Flow of Feelings, Holding, Breaking, and then Re-Membering. We found ways to love one another through the brokenness of that experience. We gathered courage from the first responders who sacrificed their lives, camaraderie from previously insignificant encounters in grocery stores, and resilience from the families who paved the way forward without their loved one present. September 11th, when The Challenger blew up, and COVID are three significant communal interruptions I've lived through in my 47 years...and there are examples of how we Re-Membered ourselves from each of these tragedies. Older generations Re-Membered through polio, World Wars I and II, and civil unrest. Future generals will Re-Member through Interruptions not yet known.

Re-Membering, like every Power of Grief, can happen on many scales. It is present in the work project that gets interrupted with a different direction, pulled funding, or escalated timeline. When this occurs, all the team members come together and assess what they've done to date (pieces of the past), the new information they are given (pieces of the present), and what options they have for a new way forward (pieces of the future). The Re-Membering can last five minutes or five months, depending on the magnitude of the project and the people involved.

That is how it is for us as individuals as well. When we find ourselves in the stage of Re-Membering, the power available on the other side of the heavy messiness is creativity. The person fired recognizes his transferable skills and secures a dream job. The woman who lived and grieved through infertility creates special bonds with nieces, nephews, and neighborhood children. The young man who fights the darkness of addiction takes all the excruciating steps to reach the light and discovers his deep sense of empathy and claims it as his superpower. The retired man finds joy in redefining his role within family and community. The woman who is actively caring for her partner in the late stages of Alzheimer's disease finds compassion in all the shattered pieces of the picture she had for her life. From the broken pieces, we are called into the creative power of Re-Membering.

During an interview with my precious and powerful friend Maria, she shared about her divorce:

"It's been a big pill to swallow...this rediscovery of who I am. And not only who I am, but who am I allowed to be? Who do I want to be? I'm carrying these new beliefs about what relationships are and what they should be and could be...and who's able to tell me what my relationship is and is not.

All of the lessons of pre-married Maria, and married Maria, and post-married Maria create someone new. That person I am becoming is who I am supposed to be! But she's never been here before so it's like creating a whole idea of what the world is now based on where I've been, what has worked, what hasn't worked, and knowing that I have a ripple effect in the world.

There's an ingenuity that comes with grief. That's just part of it. It doesn't mean it's going to be easy, but there's more available for all of us after Breaking. And there will never be a consequence for loving that cannot be restored to someone or something more beautiful."

Just as your grief is unique, so is your Re-Membering. Your re-membered self eventually becomes the new version of you. This version is not consumed with the Flow of Feelings that were the result of The Interruption. This version has released its hold and has broken into a million pieces. And, the re-membered version of yourself once again creates rhythms and cadences that accommodate who you are now, as a result of your interruption... All your interruptions.

This you is power-full.

Full of power.

And present.

And equipped for when another interruption comes.

Large or small, it is inevitable. Grief will find you. It will interrupt your cadence. It will cause your feelings to flow and create a look back that evokes holding. You will break, because that is where the light shines in. And in whatever time is required, you will create your Re-Membered self.

9

Weaving Together The 5 Powers of Grief

The 5 Powers of Grief are a new language and consideration. It may take some time to sink in and feel the gifts within these powers. Yet, with an open heart and mind, I trust these will support our culture in alchemizing grief into growth.

Let's walk through an example of what The 5 Powers of Grief look like in action.

Picture yourself in a work environment. You are in charge of a project that you have been working on for several weeks with the support of others on your team, within other departments, and outside partnerships. On a regular Thursday afternoon, you get a call from your boss. They say something along the lines of, *"The higher up's have decided to go a different direction. This project is being put on hold. They haven't said yet if we will be able to pick it back up at a later date, just that we're not to invest any additional labor or resources on it at this time. I'm sorry, I know you've put so much into this already."* **(The Interruption)**

When you hang up the phone at the end of the call, you feel......well, what don't you feel? A spike of anger, a lot of confusion, a dose of frustration, and even a pinch of relief. Your mind swirls with questions: *Was this somehow my fault? Did I not provide enough evidence of the value being produced and planned? What am I going to say to all the people who have invested in this project?*

A second wave of relief rolls in on the heels of your concern and the thought "*well, now I'll have a lot of my time back*" and "*I could see where the gaps were in this project.*"

Just as immediately, the feeling of embarrassment and the burden of unraveling it all flows in. Just as you had carefully pulled together the right people, curated the parameters of the project, and created significant headway in just a few weeks, now you must dismantle it all. **(Flow of Feelings)**

Yep, there's the anger again! Joined by what feels like a moment of paralysis. You are frozen in time as nothing seems real. You have no idea how to undue the work that's been done. *Should you send an email to everyone? Should you call each contributor? Does it need to be today, immediately...or can you sleep on it and try to have a plan formulated by tomorrow?* This project meant so much to you. It felt good to be at the helm of something important and meaningful. Now that is gone. You can't help but think of all the good it was going to create – efficiency and service. Why was this brought to a halt? Would this ever have a chance to live? **(Holding)**

You decide to reach out to your right hand person on this project. They are just a few office doors down, so you pop your head in and ask to visit for a few minutes. Behind closed doors you share about the call from the boss and your frustration, and then say, "*I don't even know what to do now.*" Your cheeks are flushed and you can feel the reality sinking in as you utter the words of not knowing what to do. Your coworker listens. They hear you. They let the air sit quiet for a moment with your final comment. Then they ask, "*Want to know what I would do?*" You stop holding your breath and your shoulders relax down from where they have been pinched up around your neck. You feel vulnerable, yet this offer of clarity from another in the moment when you feel so very lost feels truly supportive. **(Breaking)**

Whether or not you let the colleague share their ideas, you were open to support. Pretty quickly, what feels like a shattered project begins to once again take shape. It is very different from the course it was on at the start of the day. You preserve some of the existing genius already created just in case it can be picked up in the future. Then, you shut down the process and focus, for yourself and the team who have been involved. It's as if you needed your coworker to bear witness to your Flow of Feelings and to name how very unclear you were feeling in order to step into your resilience. Once again you create a path forward from this interruption. **(Re-Membering)**

This is an everyday example of The 5 Powers of Grief in action. It's a plausible, though made-up story. What is far more potent is hearing other's journeys through grief – divorce, infertility, addiction, death, diagnosis, loss of hope and dreams, loss of friendship, loss of sexual function, loss of personal identity... and on and on. Please visit KristaPowers.com to read the transcripts of interviews with some very special humans who generously share about one of their own journeys of grief. These interviews flowed organically, outside of two capstone questions at the end, so I invite you to tune in and notice words that reflect The 5 Powers of Grief within each real and raw story.

The opportunity available, should we choose to take ourselves one step further, is to proactively invite grief, specifically The 5 Powers, into our lives. Let me explain...

I'm willing to bet we have all supported or witnessed a kiddo being supported through a proactive interruption. It's called Time Out. Time out allows them to experience their flow of feelings, holding, and breaking in a safe container in order to enter back into the moment in a re-membered way. We are proactive in work settings when we call for a pause in a conversation or project and invite ourselves and teammates to assess the scenario from a different lens before forging ahead. In our pursuit of health, we walk away, rest, and refuel in the midst of repetitions or intense cardio. While far more tactical, this is another example of a proactive interruption that enables the Powers of Grief - engaged, bearing witness, presence, resilience, and creativity - to impact the moment.

There are three tools I recommend when venturing into this notion of proactively inviting and befriending grief in everyday life. The first is based on cognitive behavioral therapy (CBT) and walks through four steps to slow and assess a moment. The abbreviation is SLCA, and my friend Nan's mental trick to remember the four steps is to call it St. Louis (SL) to California (CA). I love that human!

The first step is to Stop, which is literally creating an interruption in whatever mental, emotional, physical, or spiritual chaos you may find yourself in. Admittedly, putting the breaks on or pausing can be a counter cultural act. It requires significant self-awareness, emotional intelligence, and resolve. Yet, it also does not have to be complicated. It is acceptable, and I dare say healthy, to stop when you find yourself in a whirlwind of life. The consequences of not stopping may be a burned meal, a car accident, an email sent inadvertently, a missed opportunity for a final goodbye.

The second step is Listen and Look. I like to lead with listening as I have come to realize this is a woefully underdeveloped skill in our culture. Communication is a powerful antidote to grief. Earlier, I spoke about the radical acts of asking for and receiving support, and how important they are to tapping into the powers within Breaking and Re-Membering. Without listening to ourselves and others, we are more likely to miss the mark on what is required to be whole and healthy. This step of Listening and Looking invites us into assessing the landscape of what is happening so we can proactively move to the third step, which is Choose.

These steps are incredibly simple, aren't they? They may harken the lessons we teach children before crossing the street: Stop, Look, Listen, then cross. Yet, what I have found for myself and while coaching others, is that I often miss one, two, or three of the steps and create a bigger problem for myself. If that child does not stop, they are already in the flurry of traffic and a different type of interruption is created. If they do not look or listen, they are not setting themselves up to make the best choice possible. If they do not choose - well, they miss out on a valuable life lesson that will be required in moments of crisis and calm. Without building the muscle of choice in children, we find ourselves in a sea of adults who are living life on autopilot - until interruptions happen to them and then it is a crisis.

Choosing is incredibly important. As it relates to proactively choosing grief, it may be the choice to let go of a friendship, or professional opportunity. It may be choosing to go all in on an investment or move cross country. It can mean a number of things, but the genius is in being engaged, bearing witness, being present and resilient. This is where the magic happens of a proactive interruption. When I was diagnosed with breast cancer, there was a moment I stopped, listened to my inner dialogue and Flow of Feelings, and chose to heal with and through breast cancer. I am confident this choice set me down a path that, while still challenging, was far more productive than if I had chosen a different approach such as avoidance or fear.

Finally, the fourth step is Act. Returning to the child crossing the street, if they do the first three steps and never the fourth, they simply will not get to where they want to be. I am sure you have met a person who never takes action. They may dwell in being unclear of what else is possible or their lives may appear messy. These are the heavy spaces of grief. Action can require creativity, resilience, presence and courage. Like superheroes stepping into an action scene, our powers can be put to action by practicing Stop, Look & Listen, Choose, Act. These four steps point us toward engaging with grief proactively.

The second tool I recommend for proactively inviting The Interruption, versus waiting with bated breath for it to happen to you, comes from my friend Candice. Candice has a unique perspective of grief. When she was 25, Candice intentionally decided to cut off contact with her mother. This active choice of ending an important relationship presented itself to Candice again two decades later when she decided to end her marriage of 23 years. When reflecting upon these intentional interruptions in her life, Candice came up with the acronym TRUE to encapsulate her experience of grappling with these difficult choices. With her permission, I'm happy to share this technique in case it serves you through actively inviting an interruption and grief into your life.

*"The process of identifying what is **TRUE** is strengthening my faith and keeping me grounded while I feel like my entire world is falling apart. Though I'm making the conscious but painful choice to tear down the life and relationship I have built, piece by piece, I am also dismantling lies that I believed and determining what's newly true for me in this season and stage of life.*

*Learning to **Trust** is the first step. To trust myself. It's a process of separating out and determining what's actually true, versus things I just accepted as true in the past. Though ending my marriage is one of the hardest things I've ever done, it is what is best and healthiest for me...and him too.*

***Release** is the next part of the process I am identifying. Releasing control, releasing the past, and releasing the history we had together. I've had to release the dream of our future and the comfort that came with being in something so known and familiar, even though it was unhealthy.*

*The third step is to **Understand**. Understanding my role in why my marriage was broken, taking accountability for what I contributed to it becoming toxic, and understanding the perspective of the other person in the relationship has been a huge part of my grieving process.*

*The final part of TRUE is to **Empathize**. I am learning that having empathy is where connection happens. Being able to use what I have gone through to empathize with others who have been through similar situations is where I see grief turning to gold. Empathy has layers. Grief can teach you to develop deep empathy for yourself and for others.*

Two things can be true. There are moments when I spiral in the grief I've invited into my life. There are hard and sad days. And there are glimmers of hope and inklings of the new version of myself that I really like. You can be falling apart and coming together all at the same time.

That's my high-level version of living in The 5 Powers of Grief. It's going to look different for every individual. I think it comes down to what is TRUE for you - and then Re-Membering who you are based on trusting, releasing, understanding, and expressing empathy."

As Candice and I discussed further, we identified that the E of TRUE could also stand for Embrace. Stepping into self-acceptance is a major part of leaning into the Powers of Grief. Gentle awareness and curiosity often pave a path to embracing oneself and the true picture of who you are in the midst of your grief experience. Ultimately, Candice identified that grief leads to reconnection - with self and others.

Which brings me to the final tool - actually a phrase - if you choose to proactively invite grief into your life. It was during a conversation with another powerful friend that I had a light bulb moment and really understood how to share the vision I have for how we grow into embracing grief.

Jessie is one of my primary sounding boards in life and a source of wisdom and joy. We have this ability to dive deep into conversation and heart topics and then pop up with levity and laughter. Nothing is off-limits with us! Since we met while earning our Master of Social Work degrees through a Hartford

Geriatric Fellowship scholarship, we both have a proclivity for topics related to aging, death, and dying.

While interviewing Jessie about grief wrapped into the experience of aging, we meandered off track – as we often do. Jessie told me about Al, "*a tiny, old Italian man of slight stature*" she worked with at her very first job. She was 15 and he was a World War II veteran. Although Jessie doesn't recall what they were talking about, she does remember Al saying to her, "*Adapt or Die.*" to which Jessie responded, "*well that's pretty dramatic!*" He went on to say, "*One day you'll know what I mean.*"

Revisiting this conversation three decades later via Zoom, we both giggled at first, though quickly sunk into our hearts and went still. The type of stillness that comes with peace and contentment.

I reflected, "*That is so true, real, and concrete.*" As I've written this book about grief, I have come across and had many quotes shared with me. Benjamin Franklin's quote about the two truths of life: Death and Taxes. Or Steve Jobs' quote that "*Death is the destination we all share.*" Or in other words, the common idiom, "*No one gets out alive.*" Yet, something about this conversation with Jessie really landed squarely in my heart.

I can see it playing out two different ways. One where a big, burly human barks the message: *ADAPT OR DIE!* Another where a much smaller, gentler voice speaks from a neutral tone: *Adapt or Die.* In the first, it feels looming, daunting, and dramatic with a prescribed "right answer" baked in. In the second, it feels more like an option is being placed at your feet and although you get to choose, neither is a poor choice.

That is how it is with The 5 Powers of Grief. They are all neutral by nature. They are gentle awareness and curiosity until we villainize them and attribute heaviness to each. Grief becomes a scapegoat, instead of a companion in our journey. The truth is, there is an option to be intentional with our grief and lean into the powers, just as much as there is an option to experience the heaviness. I believe the challenge is to practice reaching our arms...our minds...our hearts to both ends of the spectrum of grief, so we become whole in our experience.

Perhaps it would help to offer a visual:

HEAVY		POWER OF GRIEF		POWERFUL
Autopilot	«	**The Interruption**	»	Engaged
Consumed	«	**Flow of Feelings**	»	Bear witness
Backward Focus	«	**Holding**	»	Present
Unclear what else is possible	«	**Breaking**	»	Resilient
Messy	«	**Re-Membering**	»	Creative

Adapt or die. As it turns out, death is not the enemy. It is inevitable, both figuratively and literally. Sometimes it is necessary and time to die to a part of ourselves – a habit, a belief, a stage or age.

This calls to mind a tree along the edge of my property in the urban core of Covington, Kentucky. It was never intentionally planted, rather a seed dropped from a bird, or perhaps blown by the wind. Admittedly, I did not cut or trim it as it began growing. Within a few years, it had grown in and through the wire fence that separates my yard from my neighbor's. Its crooked and contorted trunk are evidence of adaptation. Many years later, it is fully grown and provides a corner of shade for my neighbor's dog and a portion of my property. The tree could have been stunted and ceased to grow. It could have died. Instead, it chose to thrive...to grow...to become despite the obstacle in its path. The fence could have been an interruption, but the tree simply made it part of its story.

Did you know that when there is a drought, the rings of a tree are narrower, missing, or create a false ring? These messages from trees denote not just drought, but a time of stress brought on perhaps by a pest infestation or cold temperatures. Wider rings generally indicate growth provided by ample water and favorable temperatures. And of course, like the tree on the edge of my lot, trees also bend and flex in order to continue despite what may seem like an obstacle. I think of the sidewalks buckled up as the result of tree roots, or knots in wood that represent where a branch fell off or was encased during growth. This is the tree choosing to be powerful amid obstacles and interruptions. To the tree, these interruptions do not evoke a positive or negative opportunity, rather they simply are. The tree has the option to adapt or die. Whichever it chooses just is...it is ok.

Much like the rings on a tree, our lifelines demonstrate the moments and years of ease and flow as well as the years of drought and challenge. My question to myself and to you is: *"Can I touch both the heavy and the powerful aspects of my grief? And in doing so, can I alchemize my grief into growth?"*

10

Practicing The Powers

*All revolutions start within –
you, me, each one of us.*

I continue to be wonderfully cracked open with every conversation and opportunity to bear witness to other's grief. I believe that's how it works. As we have new language and ways of relating and sharing our grief, we are permission to one another, to be engaged, bearing witness, presence, resilience, and creativity. We become permission and invitations for not only the heavy parts of grief to unfold, but also the neutral and powerful perspectives. This is how the revolution starts...or continues.

This is the practice portion of the book. In the following pages, I will share some writing prompts and visuals to help distill the messages. If you are not yet ready to practice, that is ok. It is here for you whenever and simply meant to be of support and service to you in any journey of grief.

If you are a visual learner, I want to share three ways of viewing The 5 Powers of Grief: the heavy, the neutral, and the powerful options with each Power.

First, a simple chart view, on the next page...

The 5 Powers of Grief	Heavy	Neutral	Powerful
The Interruption	Autopilot	↑	Engaged
Flow of Feelings	Consumed	↑	Bear Witness
Holding	Backward Focus	*Gentle Awareness & Curiosity*	Present
Breaking	Unclear of what is possible	↓	Resilient
Re-Membering	Messy	↓	Creative

Personally, I am drawn to visually pleasing diagrams, so my mind drafted up a circular view of The 5 Powers of Grief. In this image, The 5 Powers are presented in a swirling sort of way, representing how few straight lines exist within the journey of grief. The spiraling line becomes thicker as it continues through all five Powers, showing the heaviness of grief. The swirl feels like a downward dive into darkness, perhaps a relatable experience with grief.

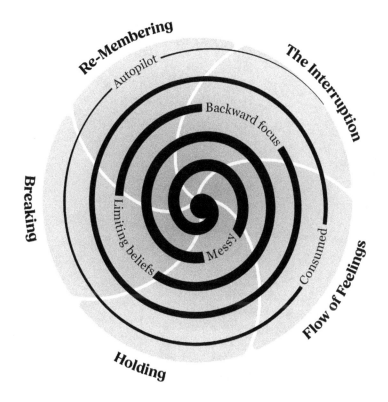

As soon as I created the visual above, I knew it needed to be shown with the powers as well. Just like grief can be both heavy and powerful, the visual gets to follow. Once again, the same information, just shared in a way that the Powers are recognized. Although there is still an experience of swirling within grief, there is an upward momentum in this image – cause for hope, possibilities, and growth.

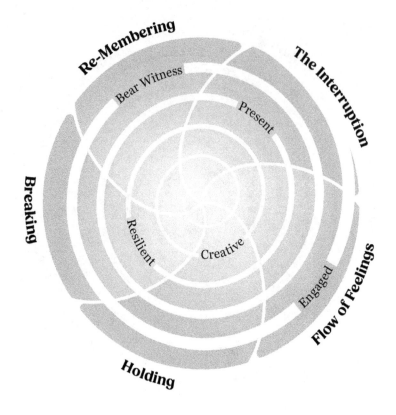

Finally, this is my favorite visual of The 5 Powers of Grief. This is sourced from my sister's love of labyrinths. She introduced me to the meditative process of this tool – not a maze, rather a one way in and one way out path that invites a person to go within and resurface again. Like grief, there are no right or wrong turns, there are many designs, and there is no pressure while walking the path. This image speaks to me of the meandering path that life takes us on, inclusive of work, play, emotions, family, community, finances, religion, politics, death and grief. Each in our own way, at our own time, we walk through all parts of our experience.

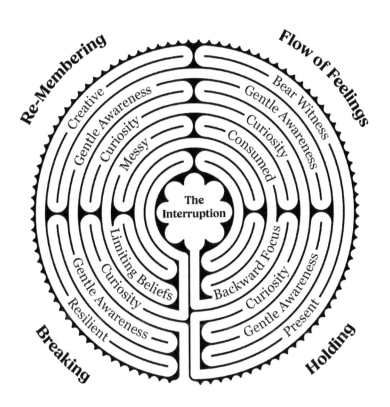

And much like life, very few things are only one dimensional.

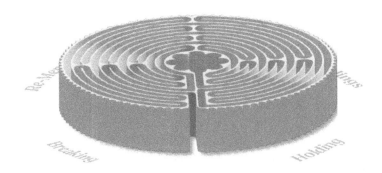

If you are one who learns best from doing, I have created writing prompts that allow you to practice The 5 Powers of Grief in relation to your own life. By spending time discerning and writing your responses to these prompts, it is more likely grief will serve as a catalyst for your growth. These may open you to additional writing and discernment which allows you to shift from the heavy to a neutral stance...and possibly all the way to the power that is available within grief.

Visit KristaPowers.com for a free downloadable worksheet

Discernment & Journaling Prompts
for The 5 Powers of Grief

Surveying the Landscape of Your Grief

1. With the recognition that grief is present in many moments (not just when a loved one dies) take some time to write a list of the losses or experiences of grief in your life.

The Interruption

2. From the list above, choose one interruption from your life to focus on for this exercise (i.e., death of loved one, divorce, loss of job, becoming an empty nester, retirement).

Flow of Feelings

3. What were some of the feelings you had at the time of this Interruption?

4. As you revisit this Interruption, what do you notice in your body now? (i.e., tight chest, jaw clenched, shoulders pinched)

5. What feelings surface now?

6. How have you or another witnessed your grief?

Holding

7. What were you most afraid of losing? (i.e., the perception of having it all together, loss of power or control, not feeling successful or organized)

8. What felt the hardest to let go of, release, or surrender?

9. What did you notice when you finally let go of that?

Breaking

10.   What was the moment/s you turned in, reflected and noticed yourself and felt still, present and aware ***and or*** the moment/s you turned out, asked for and accepted help in order to feel seen, heard, and loved?

11.   What allowed you to break your hold?

Re-Membering

12.   How have you grown?

13.   What have you stopped?

14.   What have you started?

15.   What one surprising or perhaps delightful way are you different from before The Interruption?

Deep Exploration Questions

16.   What would you say to Grief?

17.   What would Grief say to you?

If you are one who learns from reading, I invite you to explore the final part of this book: **Excerpts from A Collection of Interviews**. As previously mentioned, full interview transcripts will be shared at KristaPowers.com. The excerpts included here are the poignant, similar, and nuanced wisdom from the capstone questions poised to each interviewee.

On behalf of each person who shared, I hope you feel seen and heard in your own experience. I hope you choose to break your hold and invite support, whether that means sitting quietly with another, being held while you cry, or sharing the story of your grief for the 87th time. You are worthy of the time and space your grief requires.

11

Additional Considerations & Tools

The 5 Powers of Grief are a new perspective – one that I hope serves you, me, and many in our culture as we learn to embrace grief and invite it to be a catalyst of growth in our lives. There are several additional tools I want to offer that support the evolution of our language, understanding, and experience of grief.

Language

The language we choose and use sources from our thoughts and beliefs, and plays a powerful role in our actions, habits, and values. With that in mind, I have a small glossary of words and phrases to consider as we embrace the role grief plays in our lives. If we can adapt our language for things like vision (bifocals are now called progressive lenses) or pregnancy (pregnant women who are 35 or older used to be labeled as a geriatric pregnancy, now it is called advanced maternal age) – then we can certainly agree it is time to tune up some of the language we use with grief!

Move On

If you've ever experienced grief, you can probably feel how sticky, unrealistic and even undesirable it is to *"move on."* Yet, in our society, it's not uncommon for this language to surface. The intention may be kind – colleagues, friends, and family want us to be free of the heavy parts of grief as quickly as possible. Yet, you and I both know, moving on is not how it works! For better or worse, there is no statute of limitation with grief. The phrase I recommend replacing *"moving on"* with is *"moving through"* or *"moving with"* grief. As we soften our communication with ourselves and others, we create space for the truth of grief – it is disruptive and can linger if we do not allow ourselves to be present to it. With this language, there's less pressure to view grief as something to check off our To Do List and then proceed with little consideration of that "task" that was just "accomplished." There is no "*moving on*" as if your grief did not happen. A simple shift in words: "*move with*" or "*move through*" acknowledges and validates the ongoing process of grief, the Flow of Feelings, Holding, Breaking, and Re-Membering.

Back to Normal

In a similar vein, asking a grieving human if things are "*getting back to normal*" or if they are "*back in the swing of things*" is equally off-putting. A wise friend, familiar with grief, says "*Normal is a setting on the washing machine!*" (Thank you for this clarity, Holly Brians Ragusa!) That is to say, "normal" in relation to life is an exercise in futility.

Very likely, the human broaching the topic is equal parts courageous and hopeful you are through the heavy space of grief. Yet these questions...these words only illuminate your grief. This well-intentioned question is leading and alerts the griever that the window of time for their grief to be expressed with honesty has expired or will soon. Furthermore, going "*back*" is not possible. This language sets us all up for uncomfortable and unrealistic expectations.

My recommendation is to come from the neutral space of gentle awareness and curiosity. This allows the grieving human to reach either heavy or powerful, depending on where they find themselves in any given moment. Some examples of what this may sound like include:

- *Would you like to talk about your grief?*
- *Where are you in your grieving process right now?*
- *It seems like you are (insert emotion), do you need a listening ear?*

Avoiding the Topic or Griever

"I don't know what to say." This is one of the most common sentiments and feelings when someone we love is grieving. Between not wanting to say the "wrong" thing, to not wanting to only talk about the loss – I understand why this feeling exists. I have felt it many times myself. And so, very often, we either avoid the grieving person or don't say anything at all about their grief...which remains the elephant in the room.

My recommendation is when you feel or think *"I don't know what to say"* – reach out and say those exact words to the person you love who is grieving! If you are willing to go a step further, it can sound like this:

* *I don't know what to say and I don't expect you to guide me. I just want you to know I am here, and I care deeply about you and everything you are going through.*

Then, be there.

> Listen.
> > Pay attention.
> > > Wash the dishes or go for a walk
> > > together, or nap together....

Even when there's nothing to say, you get to say that.

I'll Pray For You

Like many, I believe in the practice and power of prayer. While I have never doubted the promise of prayers, I have wondered, *"What are you praying for specifically? Thank you, I'll take it – yet, do you even know what prayers I need and want most right now? Was this your easy way of truncating the conversation because you didn't know what else to say?"*

My recommendation is when you are inspired to say "*I'll pray for you*" to pause in that moment and actually pray out loud or in silence – Holding hands or holding your heart, eyes closed or cast up or down. Pray! In real time. It's a radical action of love and support.

What Can I Do For You?

Asking a grief stricken, exhausted human to have the wherewithal to know, prioritize, and communicate what they need is a tall order. Again, this has been a long standing, "acceptable" question to fill the space of the unknown which grief brings. Yet, this feels like one that can be retired. This question is actually quite self-absorbed – putting your own need to DO ahead of BE with the griever.

I have two recommendations:

1. Stop asking the question, "*What can I do for you?*" Instead, take some time to really notice what's missing : fresh, nourishing food? A light movie? Time for phone calls to the coroner? Yard word? Pick up and drop off of kids? Packing? Notice and show up, ready to serve.

2. Replace "*What can I do for you?*" with "*I am with you.*" Let this sink in. As basic as this notion is, it is equally stretchy...yet it shifts everything. Telling the grieving person that you are coming with as much heart (being present) as you are mind (ready to do tasks) is radically important and supportive.

Lost

While it may be controversial, I have long been curious about a common statement, "*I lost my (insert relationship/ person here)*" when a loved one dies. Without being flippant, my question has always been, "*Are they lost? Are we going to find them?*"

This is where, once again, language plays a vital role in our processing. I acknowledge that it may feel more soothing for a person to say they lost a loved one rather than directly saying they died. And, like many topics in life, I believe it is important we meet people where they are. If this is how they speak about the death of a loved one, honor that! There's no value in challenging their language in the moment, and it simply does not matter.

Yet, when you are *not* in a moment of grieving, I would invite you to explore your own relationship with death and how you talk about it. Does it feel too abrupt and stark to say someone died? Are you more comfortable with the phrase they *"passed away"*? This notion comes from 15th century England, where the belief was that a person's soul passed to another realm at the time of death. It's a softer, gentler phrase as well as more culturally aware to those who may avoid direct language about death.

The phrase I am most aligned with and believe at this point in my journey is "transitioned." My grandparents transitioned when they died. It's a bit different to say it this way at first, yet in little time it flows more easily.

Take a moment to consider what you believe. What language would best reflect your thoughts and feelings? Is that the language you use when a person dies, or have you learned to say something else and never considered it further?

On the next page is a summary of old phrases to review or retire and new options to implement individually and communally as we grieve...

Phrases to Review or Retire	»	Phrases to Practice or New Ways to BE with a Person Who Is Grieving
Move on	»	Move through / Move with
Back to Normal *Back in the swing of things*	»	Would you like to talk about your grief? Where are you in your grieving process right now? It seems like you are (insert emotion), do you need a listening ear?
Avoiding the Topic or Griever	»	I don't know what to say, and I don't expect you to guide me. *I care deeply about you and all you are going through.*
I'll pray for you	»	*Pause and Pray - in real time.*
What can I do for you?	»	Notice & Act I am with you.
Lost	»	Passed On/Away Transitioned

Write a Letter to Grief

The two capstone questions I ask at the end of every grief interview are:

What would you say to your grief?

What would grief say to you?

Most often, it causes pause. It did for me anyway. Yet, everyone who has answered these questions has done so with great heart. They spoke with tears rolling down their cheeks or a passion in their inflection. Talking to our grief allows us to immediately have a more intimate and vulnerable relationship with it... which in my experience is a pretty cool shift!

In the absence of having someone to ask and listen to your answers to these two questions, you can write a letter directly to Grief. This notion came from a wise friend. In the many years we have known each other, we have shared some truly soul-bearing truths about ourselves, as we have individually pursued the path of becoming the best version of ourselves. In a recent conversation he vulnerably shared in a journal entry. It began as a letter from Grief to him. While I have changed several aspects of this letter to honor his confidentiality, he and I both offer this as an example of how this may sound.

A Letter from Grief:

Hello it's me, your old friend Grief. I know I haven't been as good at keeping up with you as I should. You have been on my mind recently and I wanted to see if you'd be open to hanging out? We could go for a hike, have a beer... whatever. I just really want to be with you and catch up.

How have you been? Are you still hanging out with Shame

much? I know the two of you were close for a long time. Also, I talked with Loneliness the other day and he said you two try to get together quite a bit. Probably not as much as Fear and Anger... how are they by the way? They always seem so close. Their friendship is the stuff of envy. I wish you and I could spend some time becoming as close as the two of those seem to be. They seem inseparable. It's like they know each other so well they can finish each other's sentences. Two peas in a pod those guys!

I'd love to go for a long hike with you. To really catch up and spend some quality time together. We have so much to talk about. I'd like to discuss your father. His passing. His life. His absence from your life. So much that he missed out on... you! Your youth. Your fatherhood. Your marriage. Your work in the world that really mattered to others. Your siblings and their lives.

We could discuss his marriage and the damage the arguments caused. The constant tension. The violence. The rage!

I'd also like to discuss your kids. My, how they've grown! You must be proud of them for who they've become. What are their ages now? They really seem to be light years ahead of where you were at that age in many ways. It must be an odd mixture of pride and humility, of loss and gain... I know you loved being a dad - it was such a beautiful and important part of who you were... of who you still are. How are you feeling about them growing up? Moving out? Launching into their lives? I imagine you still see them as those little kids running around barefoot, playing with dolls or destroying everything in their wake. The laughter, the tears, the wrestling, and the snuggling. Watching movies, playing games, going fishing, and the nightly ritual of giving gratitude together. They are great humans because you loved them well. It's okay to admit that you miss their childhood.

What about leaving work? How has that been for you? A job you loved. A job you were really good at! You gave a lot of yourself to that organization. More than most. So many young people whose lives are richer for having you as their teacher, coach, and guide. What do you miss about being a teacher? A coach? Are there any colleagues that you miss? I imagine you miss the camaraderie. Competence, or at least feeling competent hasn't always come easy for you, I know. You could do that job with your eyes closed. It became so easy for you in many ways. But also wore on your soul. There wasn't enough challenge to inspire you to greater things. But you loved those young people well. And you taught them to seek truth, wherever it leads them, in the cause of love. You modeled humility and care, passion and purpose. They still reach out to you for advice, for help, for grace, for wisdom... that must feel good when they do. Your legacy is in all the seeds buried in the souls of people moving out into the world. Trust those seeds will be watered, nurtured, and will bear much fruit in their lives and beyond.

And coaching volleyball? You poured out your heart to your team. They saw you fight for them and defend them... so they also learned to fight for you. They can tap into that fight as they go through life and relationships, and careers. You expressed your core convictions to them on a daily basis and allowed them to begin to shape their own convictions.

God's got you!
Keep on!

What about you and Theresa? How are the two of you doing? I know your marriage has seen its share of ups and downs. So much beauty, and yet so much pain and grief as well. It's impossible that you wouldn't hurt each other. The times she hasn't seen you or heard your pain... We all fail to be compassionate at times. She can't fill that void where you've invited in Loneliness and Sadness. She has tried. She has so much fear herself that when she sees Fear in you it's too overwhelming. See her. Sit and listen to her heart. She longs for you to awaken to your strength. You've run the wrong race. Thinking you have to be something you aren't, for someone who loves you as you are. You became comfortable in a hell of your own making!

You've sat in darkness with your old friend Shame. But darkness has its own latent beauty! There is a tension in waiting for the piercing light to illuminate the darkness you and Shame share. As the Spirit hovered over the waters, so the same Spirit hovers over your soul, calling forward a new man. A whole man. One who leads with humility and vulnerability.

Share with her your griefs, your fears, your pains, your shame. She has only ever been your greatest friend, confidant, and ally in battle, but she's felt so alone and scared. Don't allow your wounds to push each other away. The light of confessing your fears brings hope, peace, and reconciliation. First, it is disruptive and painful, but it can morph into a good and useful disruption.

KEEP ON!

The invitation is to radical honesty about who you are at your core. To shed denial and politeness. To shed your passive aggressiveness. To grieve as you take an honest assessment of yourself. You are called by God to dwell courageously in truth as you wait. To name your deepest desires and harshest pains.

What are your longings?
What do you ache for?
Observe the grief you have put off for so long.

I miss you, friend. You wait for the not-yet, but you don't

*have to wait alone. Pay attention to your heart. BEHOLD!
The good thing you wait for is coming into the world. Your
world. Seek to notice one another.*

WELCOME THE STRANGER!

A Response to Grief:

Dear Grief,

*Where to begin?! I welcome your wise words. Thank you
for your letter to me! I didn't realize how much I had missed
you. Your letter has haunted me with hope and inspired
me to explore those themes with courage. Thank you for
the invitation to dwell in turbulent waters together.*

*It is true, Fear and Anger, Loneliness and Shame have all
been faithful friends to me for as long as I can remember.
But I'd like to grow beyond those friendships and explore
new terrain with some healthier allies.*

*I've been sitting with your words and allowing them to
penetrate deeply into my heart. I have a lot of questions
about some of your thoughts:*

*Why do Fear and Anger hangout together?
What is the dynamic between them that keeps them so close?
Does Anger protect Fear?
Is Anger the tough guy protecting Fear from being seen?
What is Fear protecting?*

*I want to be able to welcome both without judgment and
give them a voice, a place at the table where they can be
seen and heard.*

My relationship with Shame feels more complex, deeper

than I even know. He wants to hide and wants me to hide with him. He's lonely and doesn't want me to leave him in the dark, but he's also afraid of the light.

You were so wise to bring up the four areas you did! My father, my kids, my previous job/career, and my wife. You're right to address those areas and I welcome your presence and perspective in those areas and relationships...in all areas. Your letter has me wondering what other areas do I need your wisdom to penetrate and give me counsel?

My father really did miss out on SO much...so much life! I'm beginning to see how it is primarily a result of not having an openness to a deep relationship with you that caused him to miss out on so much. He really could have benefited so much from your friendship. He carried so much heartache and loss. His relationship with Shame seems to have been more complex than mine. He and Anger were not strangers at all. In fact, I think for him Anger was protecting Shame more than Fear. Anger would show up so often and had no issue being seen! I would get so scared around him. I really began to hate his presence because it seemed that when he was there everyone suffered - my father, and my siblings especially. Anger would suffocate Shame and not let him be seen and known. It's like he had to have the spotlight.

Thanks for bringing up my kids! They truly bring me so much JOY! And yes, I have loved being their Dad, and I love it still. I feel kind of lost at this point though as their dad. Maybe - I think sometimes - that because they are so grown - that they no longer need me. As if they've developed beyond my capacity to provide them with anything of value. What can I give them at this point? I was so sad when Jordan left for school. Like a massive piece of my own heart was gone. Same with Collin. I need to be a steady presence for Joshua when Anger comes over to hang out with him. Actually, today Jordan started an internship where she will be for 2 months. I couldn't be more proud of her! They are all so unique... uniquely gifted and uniquely flawed. What a mystery it all is!!! Our lives are this mysterious gift to one another and, like my mom, I've often allowed others like Anger or Shame to dictate the way I show up in my life. Is it possible to break those co-dependencies? To live as a free man? As a wise soul, unafraid to love, to be loved, to be seen and known in all my messiness and glory? I definitely miss their childhoods. They were so much fun... and so much work! But that work gave me such a deep sense of purpose and meaning, and now that they are grown I sense a deep void of purpose and meaning.

Adding to that void, leaving a career I loved and excelled at has been overwhelming so I tried to avoid the feeling of emptiness and instead of inviting you to sit with me I pushed you away. I see now what a profound mistake that was, and how your absence caused so much suffering in my heart and the lives of others I love most.

Dear Grief, please forgive me for pushing you away. I know now what a gift you are to me, and what need I have of you being a faithful presence in my life. You are so welcoming of the parts of me I've tried to put off and forget. You hold as sacred those mysterious depths that I've been too afraid to explore and bring light to. You have held out hope for healing and wholeness where I've only known despair and terror.

Teaching and coaching was to me the integration of all my known skills, competencies, and aspirations. I did love it, and I was very good at it. I wanted to leave that place better than I found it. I don't know about the place, but I do believe I left my students and athletes better. I do miss the camaraderie. The relationships with young people who are now adults are very fulfilling to me. I do enjoy it when they reach out to me. I love hearing where their lives are going and what they hope to do in the world.

Theresa, thank you for bringing her up in your letter. What a divine gift she is to me. It's been a tremendously difficult season in our relationship, and I can't help but conclude that it is at least partly because I have pushed you away rather than welcome you to the table of our relationship, our marriage, and home. She is simply the most extraordinary person I've ever known...and she always has been that in my mind. But I'm not sure that pedestal is fair of me. I have idealized her to such a degree that I haven't loved the incarnation of her in real life...at least I haven't loved her well enough to allow her the very freedom I long for myself. Why can't I just allow her to be as she is in the very moment of presence without placing on her the unbearable burden of filling every void in my own soul? She is not my savior! I so desperately want her to be my best friend and I hers. But the pedestal upon which I've placed her won't allow me to be her equal, her partner, her friend. Damn! I've hidden from her the very thing I long for her to have... my own heart.

My old friend Fear doesn't mind being present when I'm talking with close friends - I can articulate my inner world with great detail even with Fear sitting beside me. But when I am talking to Theresa about my inner world, Shame or Anger seem to want to dominate the conversation. Why is this? Her beauty, her soul, her light, her magnificent heart feel overwhelming to me! She is shrouded in light, mystery, beauty, and ancient wisdom that touches a deeply young place in me. Even after 29 years of marriage I still feel like a 15 year old boy at a total loss for what to say or do - or how to be. Where is the man? Where did he go? He shows up sometimes, but more times than not he is nowhere to be found. Like my mom, he has disappeared when he is most needed. His presence, his gifts, his wisdom, his perspective, his strength...all are needed but seem to have fled in the face of beauty he'll never understand or embrace. So Anger and Shame steal the show in the vacuum created by his absence. I've wounded her so deeply and Shame never lets me forget all the ways I've failed her. To be the man she needs, wants and deserves.

Dear Grief, help me! Help me be fully present to her. She is the love of my life. Can you lend me your wisdom? Can you coach me to show up for her...for myself, for her...I long to be fully with her the rest of my days. To be the man she wants, the man she can be fully herself with...help me not to shrink when she gets angry, sad, or stressed. Help me to be her anchor, her safe harbor, a rock upon which she can rest. How do I become that?

You encouraged me to "keep on"...I'm going to adopt that as my own motto. I'm practicing the things you so generously challenged me with:

Radical honesty
Shed politeness and denial
Grieve boldly my losses
Name my deepest desires and harshest pains
To ask myself what I truly long for. What I ache for.

I hope you and I are able to hangout more...to hike together, to have that beer. You help me see myself and the mystery of this life with so much more clarity and wisdom. I've needed your presence more than I could have imagined. You encouraged me to pay attention to my heart...I don't know how to do that other sitting in silence and writing... I'm open to suggestions if you have them...I'm done with ignoring our relationship.

Toward the end of your letter you told me to BEHOLD! - I'm sitting with that...not entirely sure what it means. To take in and taste the beauty of this life in all of its mystery and heartache. There seems to be a deep connection between beauty and pain, between mystery and longing. Hope and desire. Maybe we need more poets than politicians. What did you mean by "Welcome the stranger"? You and I have been estranged... is it you? I've kept Theresa at arms length... is it her? Could it be all the exiled parts of myself that I've ignored in order to be with Anger, Shame and Fear?

Sit with me my friend. I welcome you.

Pretty powerful, right? I feel deeply intrigued by the closeness I feel reading this...the collegial sense between me and grief. Consider taking some time to listen. Ask Grief to speak to you. Ask it what it wants to say. Then, bear witness to Grief. Listen and write it down. You may be amazed at what surfaces.

During another interview, my friend Megan shared about her grief through infertility. Without being prompted, at the end of our time together, Megan spoke this message to the children she never birthed. It's another option for your own gentle process.

To the kiddos that I would have had,

I would have absolutely loved you. I would have loved being your mom. I would have loved sharing you with Izzy. Seeing the way she is with Lollie...for God's sake... the way she is with our nieces and nephews! I would have loved seeing her wake you up in the morning, and the delight in your faces when you saw either of us or Lollie.

Maybe in a past life...maybe I was such a mother, and it carried over in the next life. I hope to have that in another life. But in this life, I'm so fortunate. We host and celebrate and spoil our friends and their children. We really are so blessed.

I just started a new chapter of life, a new job. And I think, like my mom used to say, "it's never too late to reinvent yourself." So I will continue to reinvent what I thought I was going to be...and I will probably have to do it again. For whatever reason, I wasn't made to be a biological mother. I have been mothered well, and I have other people and things that I get to care for and love and see grow. Yet, I still have a little piece in my heart – a little hole and it doesn't ever need to be filled. That is you in my heart.

I love you.

To Megan, Izzy, and my tender friend who shared his letters with Grief...thank you. Thank you for teaching me...for modeling to so many of us. Namaste.

~~~~~~~~~~~~~~~

Resurrection Dates

Anniversaries are important. They are mile markers along life's road trip that we celebrate and remember, signifying mountain top and valley moments. Hallmark has capitalized on anniversaries of birth and weddings. They have expanded into other milestones of graduating from one experience to another – including school graduations, work promotions, and retirement. And of course they have cards of sympathy.

Yet, what about all the anniversaries that roll around on an annual basis of the hard moments? The diagnosis date, the divorce decree, the day our loved one died. These moments may feel forgotten, except for the ones most closely impacted by The Interruption. I suspect even if we do remember, much like not having the words in the moment, the cyclical reliving leaves us equally at a loss as to how to best support someone we love who may find themselves grieving in a more pronounced way on a heavy anniversary.

We now have language and additional tools to grow into (above), and I want to introduce another idea. My recommendation is to keep a calendar of Resurrection Dates and grief milestones. My dad is the wise one who created the Resurrection Date idea – a simple word document with the person's name and date of death. Every day during his morning ritual, he pauses to honor whoever may be listed as dying on that day in the past. Often, he'll send a text to the remaining family to let them know they are being thought of on this tender day.

This harkens the quote used in Disney's movie *Coco*, "*They say you die twice. Once when you stop breathing, and a second time, a bit later on, when somebody mentions your name for the last time.*" Whether this quote is attributed to the ancient Egyptians, French literature, Ernest Hemingway, or Banksy, the sentiment is what's important. It's simple and profound. A practice of Resurrection Dates allows us to continue uttering the names of those we have loved, so they only die their first death.

To some, this may seem overwhelming and grief-filled to have such a list. What my dad has realized through this practice is that collective grief can be a pathway to deeper peace. He shares, "*This grief does not contain the intense grief of an individual event. Rather it contains an overview of all the lives that have touched my life and helped form me. The list has been compiled over the last 25 years and reflecting upon it, there are more persons in Resurrection to welcome me home than there will be at my funeral. It is amazing how it has shifted and mellowed my vision of my own death.*"

His list often has more than one name on a given date, yet with different years of death. My dad is able to reflect on multiple names on any given day or month and view these souls as a team. He ponders, "*What would it have been like if they met each other?*" He is able to reflect upon each one's influence in his life. "*From this I have learned, those who have died still have gifts to bestow upon me throughout my life. The collective grief fueled through their spirits and memories provides me with comfort and love.*"

The practice of recording Resurrection Dates is an act of communal reflection. It has the power of peace wrapped within it, should you choose to engage.

Why Wait?

Have you ever paused to notice how easy it is to say endlessly loving things to a baby? We coo over the rolls of fat on their legs, delight in their laughter, and find comfort in sharing the quiet moments as they sleep. Or, how encouraging we are to children as they utter their first word, take their first step, create art, and on and on? Science shows that positive affirmations improve mental and emotional health. Affirmations boost self-esteem, reduce anxiety, and promote resilience.

Yet, there is a vast "in between" that exists from saying the things to little humans and waiting until (hopefully) decades later when a person dies to once again reflect on and celebrate all that we love about the person who is no longer with us.

These realities are why I chose to create something new. All of us could benefit from a dose of resilience and a decrease of anxiety! So, **Why Wait?** It's time to say the things and celebrate the human at any age and stage of life...here and now!

Why Wait? is a custom created experience that celebrates humans at any stage and age of life. It was born from:

- the feelings inspired at a couple powerful memorial services and funerals;
- a deep belief in and practice of acknowledging humans for their gifts and presence; and,
- a dream of revolutionizing our cultural norms around living and dying.

It is far easier than we believe to speak acknowledgements and show appreciation for the people in our lives. **Why Wait?**

transforms thoughts and feelings into tangible messages to those we love most. Through the support of guided questions and templates, a life-affirming experience is easily woven together to create a radical act of love and celebration for a special human.

While this idea is not difficult, it is out of the norm. If you are curious about creating a **Why Wait?** celebration for someone you love – including yourself – please visit KristaPowers.com.

Other Resources

Earlier, I shared the quote, *"None of us are getting out of here alive."* This is attributed to Nanea Hoffman who went on to say, *"so please stop treating yourself like an afterthought. Eat delicious food. Walk in the sunshine. Jump in the ocean. Say the truth that you're carrying in your heart like hidden treasure. Be silly. Be kind. Be weird. There's no time for anything else."*

Powerful, right? And it's the first line of Hoffman's quote that deeply resonates and makes the idea of death a bit more palpable for me. We are all going to die eventually. With this in mind, I wanted to offer a few additional resources that are ideally accessed well before we are ailing. Life is now! Take some action so your future self, and the circle of support around you, is clear about what you need and want at the end of your life.

Professional Experts

While resources are readily available at our fingertips at all times through the worldwide web, I cannot implore you strongly enough to find a trusted, local professional in the industry of aging, dying, and planning. I highly recommend opening the conversation with your circle of support to find out if they have someone they could refer you to. I would also point everyone in the direction of an Elder Law Attorney. Whatever your age may be, this is the professional skilled at supporting you in setting up health directives, estate, and end of life plans. Read reviews online and take time to find someone you feel comfortable with as you traverse what may feel like a big, foreign matter.

The Grief Recovery Handbook by Russell Friedman and John W. James

As highlighted in Chapter Two, The Grief Recovery Handbook is a working tool for any kind of loss or experience of grief. It offers practical steps for healing through and after a loss.

Did I Forget to Mention by Barb Markey

Did I Forget to Mention is a book like no other. It is a living document. A collection that will benefit you and your loved ones. It is an account of critical information; a place to keep the passwords of your life, letters to loved ones, monthly bills, accounts, important dates and addresses... all in one place.

The Rabbit Listened by Cori Doerrfeld

A children's book with a message for all ages, graciously gifted to households across the country thanks to Dolly Parton's Imagination Library.

My Friend – I Care by Barbara Karnes

Access this and many other short, supportive books about end of life education at bkbooks.com.

Speaking Grief at pbs.org

A 57-minute PBS documentary that *"explores the transformative experience of losing a family member in a grief-avoidant society. It validates grief as a normal, healthy part of the human experience rather than a problem that needs to be 'fixed.' It also addresses the role that support from friends and family plays in a personal grief experience, offering guidance on how to show up for people in their darkest moments."*

The Colors of Love and Loss by Dr. Joanne Cacciatore

This book helps children navigate grief. It is available for free in both English and Spanish at MISSFoundation.org

The Conversation Project an initiative of the Institute for Healthcare Improvement

Information about National Healthcare Decision Day and other free resources to help people share their wishes for care through the end of life. Visit theconversationproject.org.

You are not alone. Asking for and receiving support through your grief will be one of your most beautiful and radical acts of self-love.

Send Off Thoughts

As we come to an end, there is no way for me to know what has been stirred within you while reading this book. Just as I began, I want to conclude – not so much with my intention or dream, rather with the request that I put forth in the early pages: That you trust. Trust you are where you need to be. If you are not at ease, trust that this is not where you will be forever. Please trust yourself and whatever process you are craving here and now. I choose to trust that something from these pages shined light on the darkness you have or are feeling. And I trust that as we engage our grief, we will come to know it has so much power to share.

There's a litany called Ancestral Mathematics that I once saw while scrolling on social media. It resonates every time I read it. It goes like this:

Ancestral Mathematics

In order to be born, you needed:
2 parents
4 grandparents
8 great-grandparents
16 second great-grandparents
32 third great-grandparents
64 fourth great-grandparents
128 fifth great-grandparents
256 sixth great-grandparents
512 seventh great-grandparents
1,024 eighth great-grandparents
2,048 ninth great-grandparents

For you to be born today from 12 previous generations, you needed a total of 4,094 ancestors over the last 400 years.

Think for a moment – How many struggles? How many battles? How many difficulties? How much sadness? How much happiness? How many love stories? How many expressions of hope for the future did your ancestors have to undergo for you to exist in this present moment?

Although our families may look different today than 400 years ago, the message is still clear. Our very existence required hundreds and thousands of other people. Our deepest grief – whether heavy or powerful – paves the way for others who are with us now and are yet to be born. Grief is woven through our lineage and is part of being whole.

Be gentle with yourself, you beautiful human.
Bear witness to yourself, and others.
Get present.
Take yourself on.
You are resilient and creative!

Excerpts from A Collection of Interviews

While writing **Good Grief**, **I was excited** – excited by the possibility to share and be of service to anyone who may be grieving and to our cultural norms around grief. In the final two months of writing this book, I decided to interview a handful of humans about their experiences of grief. As soon as that process began, **I was in love**. That is what co-creation is – it's being in love and creating something exponentially greater. I have no doubt; these stories will reach further and dive deeper into hearts than my book could have done without them. It is my greatest honor to learn from these humans, and so many others, as we traverse the grief and joys of life.

The full transcript of each interview will be posted on KristaPowers.com. Each interview flowed and unfolded uniquely, except for two capstone questions I asked at the end. Below are excerpts from these interviews in response to the questions:

What would you say to Grief?

And what would Grief say to you?

While these interviews were focused out, there was one who whittled her way in and gently, though with great intention, asked, "*So Krista, have you answered your own questions yet? What would **you** say to grief?*" I took a deep breath and then...wept.

It is an honor to share my response, as well as so many others below. They are insightful in the similarities, and stimulating in their differences. May you read and receive each of these beautiful and raw responses with gentle awareness and curiosity. May you feel seen and supported. We (the universal and greater "We") are with you.

By the way, thank you for letting me enter into this process in such a vulnerable way – you know who you are.

Krista Powers

What would you say to Grief?
I'd sit with you Grief, and cry for a while...
I feel you. I feel why I've needed you. I feel that you've meant no harm.
I'm sorry I've pushed you away.
Please forgive me for not always wanting you.
Thank you for always being present.
I love you.

What would Grief say to you?
I don't think She would say anything.

There are two gestures I do that I think She would do...I don't know if I learned them from Her, or if I'm projecting myself onto grief. I think She would hold her hands in a gentle, open way like this (gestures with palms facing up, as if ready to hold something placed in them). I think She would hold her hands like this...like the gentle embrace that is available when you just want to be held. Not tight – just open and available for me when I need to rest.

And then like this (gestures with hands up and palms facing out around shoulder height). As if to say either "Praise be!" or "Yeah, keep going!" or "This is holy, this is well." I think that is how She would respond.

Jackson Athey, Grief through addiction

What would you say to Grief?
I would say thank you. I think grief and love are similar in a lot of ways. It is such a powerful teacher. I think it is misunderstood in many ways too. But, the main thing I would say is, 'Thank you for making me stronger and for helping shape me into who I am today.'

What would Grief say to you?

I'm not sure what Grief would say to me. I feel like it would look at me with admiration for how I've dealt with it. If it had any words to say it would be, 'You've done well so far, but you have a long way to go and there will be much more of me to deal with. We will see how you do then.' Kind of proud but also weary of what's to come and how I will deal with it when that time comes.

Jessie Cybrowski, Grief within aging

What would you say to Grief?

That question makes me speechless...
I think I would say, Grief, you are a formidable opponent and a formidable companion. You have made me who I am. For that, I am grateful. I could see a little less of you, but I also feel like I am learning to be a better version of me. It also bears stating that I'm still figuring out how to live with you. Some days are easier than others. Lately I hate your guts but also, I don't hate your guts sometimes...because it's who you are.

It's funny to personalize grief into someone I can talk to. It makes me struggle for words, because I recognize that what grief is coming with is what grief is...it's not for me to challenge what one is. So I have to learn to appreciate grief for grief. So when grief makes me mad or sad, that's on me, and I need to just figure out how to move past those feelings that limit me in relation to grief and find what works for me in relation to grief.

In a funny way, I almost would say to grief, 'bear with me.' Bear with me while I figure out how to interact with you, because I know that we're lifelong partners in this gig. So just bear with me.

What would Grief say to you?

Oh God, Grief would say something obnoxious like, 'I

wouldn't give you more than you could handle' (said snidely). It would say something like, 'everyone goes through it.' And I would throw my hands up and be like, 'What the fuck?'

Grief has a fucking sick sense of humor – a dark sense of humor, which is necessary. It has Gallows humor, which I'm actually quite sensitive to. I try not to use Gallows humor. I think ultimately, Grief would say something dark and flippant right to my face, but then She would be like, 'Let's go,' and we would walk together. I think of grief, the way some people imagine the Grim Reaper, but with just slightly softer imagery. There's no sickle, probably equally dark and slightly ominous in presence, but again, almost like that evil character that you get to know and you almost begrudgingly like. Grief has been made a villain, and as it turns out, she's just been a scapegoat the whole time. She's our good friend. She loves us so much. She's always there to teach us something and to help us grow...and we're mad at her or pushing her away. She's resilient though and she always comes back. She's urgent when she needs to be urgent, and she's patient when she needs to be patient. She really gets it right.

Thank you, Grief, for coming to visit me. For showing me what I'm capable of, for teaching me the depths of my ability to love. For allowing me to fall so deeply in love to understand the power of humanity. And how to appreciate life.

Nan Fischer, Grief through the journey of Alzheimer's with a partner

What would you say to Grief?
You sneaky little bastard!

And I think I'd say too, it's like you're everywhere. Everywhere, every day. You are not just there for the big ticket times. You are here every day in so many ways. You are probably the most unexplored emotion in humans. You

are the most avoided and least understood, for good reason. And you are very pervasive and very demanding of our attention. Like, ignore it at your own peril!

What would Grief say to you?
Well now that I've got your attention...

I'm glad you finally have learned more about me. I'm glad you've learned that I am here every day and ignore me at your own peril. Martha Beck has a great emotional compass chart in her book Finding Your Own North Star. It talks about the four main emotions – fear, anger, joy and grief. She says the way to get through grief is to work with it and give up your illusion of permanence. It is an illusion that things are permanent, and ironically, in later life, one of Rose's favorite expressions was. 'The only thing permanent is change.'

Patrick Flerlage, Grief related to being fired

What would you say to Grief:
Fuck off...!?

Grief is just so funny. It covers so much and is such an umbrella term. You know when you say grief, the first thing that pops into people's head is a funeral, but it also has meaning related to the loss of something undefined – like a job. And then it can trickle down into grief in the loss of yourself and your identity and then that fans out into the loss of friendship and the loss of what you felt was what you were meant to do. And then the fear that sets in of 'how am I going to support my family now?' So it's like I want to give grief a big old middle finger. With it being so multifaceted and how my brain works, I end up having task paralysis. Like, where do I start? It feels like the glass has been shattered, and you have to put it back together. And how do I do that, because it can be a spiraling vortex of shit sometimes!. I'd say grief is like cockroaches when it comes to job loss. You're constantly fumbling around the dark, but once you turn the light on, the grief goes away. Once that light of 'What do you want to do?' got turned on, the grief went away...the stress went away... and I was able to walk into an interview and confidently say, 'I'm going to be the best thing that has happened to your office in the last 15 years.'

What would Grief say to you?

After me telling it to fuck off? This is where it sucks because the feeling of grief is like a leech that is in a spot where you can't reach and it's just sucking your happiness, your self-worth, your confidence, your sleep... So, it feels like with that reaction from me telling it to fuck off, and how it's made me feel, that the easy answer would be that grief is just trying to pull me down, and it's telling me 'No, no, no, you are worthless. You are replaceable. You are a mere cog in the wheel, and no one cares.'

But without grief, you're an emotional automaton that can just go job to job to job and have no connection. Without grief, you never have that moment of introspection of, 'What did I do to contribute to this?' And then, 'How can I grow at my next job? How can I prevent what just happened from happening again...or take what I've learned and get a better job, higher pay, higher esteem, or whatever?' You can't have a mountain without a valley. Grief is your valley. Your dream job or your vocation is your mountain. So, you must have grief. I had to have that loss to realize how good I had it, or to know what I did not want at my next job – whether that's something about how management is or something within yourself that you have to work on.

Grief is such a vital part of life. It's like a weighted blanket. Yeah, it's a lot to carry, but it also keeps you warm. There's a certain quietness with grief that is there to remind you that this sucks. This sucks a lot, but you're gonna get through it. No matter what those other voices say and scream and yell, there's a reason that you have to go through it. You have to know the light and the dark. You have to know the heavy and the light and it comes in there with that weighted blanket to remind you this is heavy.

But also, that weight is like a protective shell. It gives you a moment or some time to go, 'I'm okay. It sucks, but I'm okay.'

And that is what Grief tells me on repeat, 'This sucks, but it's okay. This sucks and you're gonna get through this.'

When you land a job, that's when the blanket starts to slip off. You come out of that shell and that cocoon, and you're okay. You plant your feet and the mantra shifts from 'This sucks, but you're going to be ok' to 'I'm okay.' And you eventually put the blanket down and realize, 'That sucked, but I'm ok. That is behind me now and what remains of me is ok.'

That's the whisper. Grief is a whisper. Grief is the partner. It sticks with you and in time it shifts to past tense: That sucked and you are okay. Then it asks, 'what are you gonna do?' And you remember, recreate, recentering with all the shattered pieces that the light shines through.

Lacey Fox, Grief as a funeral director

What would you say to Grief?
The first thing that comes to my mind is 'Be gentle with me' because grief is such a roller coaster.

What would Grief say to you?
I'm sorry....you just have to go through it.

Anne Gerber, Grief through her mother's health decline and death

What would you say to Grief?
Go away and come back another day. I don't know. I mean, grief is just not something you embrace. Maybe I should, I don't know.

What would Grief say to you?
I think Grief would say it's okay to cry.

I don't know if I cried enough. I mean, I cried when she died, and then I just had to plan all the details of her funeral. I had to make her video. I had to make her casket panel. I had to look through all the pictures and get them on boards. It was a lot.

And so I think having a good cry is important. I had a good cry this weekend, where I just stopped, and that felt good. I think it's good to show your emotions.

Grief would say, Sit with me and cry for a while.

Kris Girrell, Grieving the loss of physical and sexual function

What would you say to Grief?
It's not so much what I would say to grief, it's what I would ask her, "Great teacher, what is it that I must still learn?"

What would Grief say to you?
She whispered, "Humility."

Elizabeth Huffman, Grief through motherhood and
possible diagnosis for child

What would you say to Grief?

I would say that I wish it would be clearer and that I could have had time to understand it more. I wish that I could have had a conversation with it before the kids to ask what I could expect from it? What does it need from me? How can I make this an easier process for the both of us? For some time I would have said, 'I'm mad at you for ruining my perfect baby.' But now, because I've gotten my head around it a little bit, and since we don't have a lot of answers and I know how many outcomes there can be...I can push back on grief a little bit. I can say, 'That's fine and I accept the fact that you're going to be here making fun of me for a few years. Also, you can stay in your place while you do that, and let me get on with my life while I accept that I have to live with you for a while. I can live independently-ish from you while we do this and figure it out.'

What would Grief say to you?

Tough shit? I laugh, but I feel like that's what Grief would say to me. I think that it would tell me that if it had any answers for me, it would have told me. It would say that we have to figure it out – maybe the hard way – together. Why? Because the days are so uncertain, I don't know what's gonna happen each day when we wake up. I don't know what developmental stage my kids have decided that they've hit. I just feel like grief doesn't really care about your feelings necessarily. Grief is not a feeling that wants to give back to you. It's not love, or it's not care, it's not fulfillment, it's a feeling that is just kind of a rock bottom thing. There's no gain for grief to give back to you, and there's no reason for it to help you reconcile it. So, I just kind of feel like grief is one of those things that would just be like, 'Oh, you're sad. Well, all right. Well, let's figure it out.' I feel like the reason we have other emotions that help us with grief is because grief doesn't itself propel you from grief. I think grief is fine. Holding you. It gives it something to do and someone to be with.

Stephen McIntosh, Grieving the loss of hopes and dreams

What would you say to Grief?

Oh, I would say to grief, you've had your place and you were needed, but now you've met your expiration date. Grief has to have an expiration date – at every stage.

I would say, Thank you so much. Thank you for your service. Thank you for letting me know that something was wrong. It's like, if something's wrong in my body and it gives me pain. Thank you pain for letting me know that something is not right so I can fix it.

Thank you for making me realize that I'm still human. Hmm. We forget our humanity sometimes, and grief comes in and be like, Hey!

Grief makes you compassionate. Grief makes you...if you allow it...stronger and wiser. Discernment comes out of grief. You know, if you keep sweeping it under the table, you're never going to move on. And how are you going to be able to not just be a beacon for other people, but a beacon for yourself? I was holding on to things from college that were negatively affecting me on my jobs. At some point I said, Okay - you're still stuck there.

What would Grief say to you?

I think Grief would say to me, I'm always here if you need me...just know that. I will be here.

Tammy Miller-Ploetz, Grief as a hospice Social Worker as well as her own mother's death

What would Grief say to you?

The first thing that comes to mind is "you suck!"

I say it's like childbirth, that you can't really understand the feeling and the depth of it until you experience it yourself.

Trying to put into words these really complex feelings is challenging and scary. I would tell my grief to try to be more convenient, to not get in the way of me living a healthy and productive life. I would tell my grief that it is closely attached to the inner child and although it is not childish it elicits feelings that are very basic and elementary. I would tell grief that I can appreciate the ebb and flow within the process and that the process is never ending. The waves on a beach come high and they come low, but they always come...sometimes stronger than other times. Grief is seasonal in many ways. I tell my clients that it is unrealistic for us to walk through our lives being completely overtaken and stifled because of our grief. We need to find ways of engaging and participating in our worlds and our relationships. It doesn't mean that we don't always have the grief or the feelings, but we need to find a place where they can rest comfortably so that we may function in a way in which we need.

What would Grief say to you?
I think this is an interesting concept and I think throughout our lives grief does speak to us and teaches us and shows us so many things about life and how we live and how we interact with each other.

I think my own grief would tell me to be patient. My own grief would tell me that the level of pain and loss that we feel is directly proportional to the love that we've experienced. My grief would tell me to allow myself the opportunity to be vulnerable and sad and reflective. My grief would also tell me that it's okay to have so many different feelings at once. It would tell me to recognize that although I am grieving and experiencing a huge loss, there is an opportunity for change that may not be apparent immediately yet does come down the road. My grief has taught me the dread and fear of someday causing this type of pain to my own children. There's nothing I would want more than to be able to mitigate their pain and loss throughout life and it is a futile effort to think that it's possible. I always felt that the loss of my mother was exacerbated because the one person who would help me through the loss and these feelings would be the person who I'm grieving. Perhaps this is one of life's great ironies when you experience the loss of someone you love deeply. My grief would remind me to accept invitations and say yes and embrace new and different and scary. Time is not an unlimited commodity, and our Human Experience is finite. My grief would tell me that it is valuable and worthwhile and important to walk through as an individual and as a community. Grief is meant to be shared, and it is through the shared Human Experience that we can find Healing.

Megan Mitchell, Grief through infertility

What would you say to Grief?
Thank you and fuck you. And, you're a bitch. You're so sneaky.

What would Grief say to you?
Grief should probably say, "I'm still here." I think grief would say, "Thank you for getting it and for helping other people with some of their grief. Thank you for being able to hold space for people with grief.

Yeah, Grief would say, I'm not going anywhere. I'll probably come back.

And this grief comes when I go to a niece's or nephew's wedding. This grief comes when I see the neighborhood kiddos that we've helped, you know like when they graduate or move out. But luckily, we've built a community where we can share some of that. So I know we can cry with each other. I think grief would also say, be aware of it. Don't let it ever get totally down. It would say, I'm here to test you and to work through some things with you, but I'm not here to end you. I think that's us telling ourselves: oh, grief will kill me. This grief could kill me. Yes, it can, if you let it. And that's not to say that someone is stronger or weaker or whatever. It's about being able to deploy the necessary resources and steps to get out of your mind because grief tells you things that are not always correct. I mean, sometimes you are in PTSD mode and your brain is functioning at a different chemical level. In those times you have to really say, Wait, I need to go do some yoga right now. I need to go for a walk. I need to sweat. I need to not eat a bunch of sugar, I need to talk to someone who is a professional. Maybe it means you're on medication for a period of time through your grief. It may be required to save your life! You should not NOT take an antibiotic when you have strep throat. You don't not use a crutch when you break your leg. These are things that are put in our paths to help. If there's somebody out there that is grieving too much or too hard, those are the people that I want to find and tell them that they can get through this.

Michele Mischler, Grief through the journey of Alzheimer's with a partner

What would you say to Grief?

I would say grief is a necessary part of life. You know, bad things happen to good people. I don't know that you ever get through it, from the readings I've done, the people I've talked to, and the thoughts I've given it. It's been said, 'You've got to go through it. You can't try to climb over or around it.' I don't think you're ever done with grief. It's just different over time. Something will pop up in a way that I wasn't expecting. But it's not necessarily a bad thing. There's sadness in life …it's just a part of life.

What would Grief say to you?

It was different than I thought it would be. I'm not a shed a tear kind of person, but I can feel really deeply. Grief moves with me. Everything I've kept in this space is a memento of something we had done or shared – I didn't buy anything new. I look around and think, 'I was so lucky to have shared that with Bill.' This space, and maybe grief, feels like an embrace…like your home has become a little hug.

Dianne Powers, Grief through her mother's death

What would you say to Grief?

We're as big and as strong and as depthful as grief is, it's evidence of how big and strong our love is. In spite of it being so very, very, very hard, I have to remind myself, it's the loss and the lack of that love, and to remember that it's a blessing. I'm glad that I'm hurting this hard, because that assures me that my love was that true and that deep. So bring it on.

What would Grief say to you?

Dianne, you're going to be ok with me. I've got you, you know I'm here. I'm part of your human life, embrace, befriend me. Pray. Ask God to help you. Ask for help and be open. I know you know I will never go away. Be with me. I can help you learn, see light and become more you. Please, come to some peace with me.

Thom Powers, Grief within retirement

What would you say to Grief?

In my men's work, I have fallen in love with the phrase "to befriend it." Grief is an invitation to learn and by befriending it, it does not grow out of control into a Monster.

What would Grief say to you?

I think grief would say to me that by staying out of your head and going deeper, I have brought you the gift of learning about compassion.

Lindsey Simons, Grief as a child graduates high school

What would you say to Grief?

I feel like, as much as I don't want it to happen, grief has been a beautiful lesson...and actually a beautiful experience too. Grief has taught me so much about the person I'm losing and also about myself. It has helped me reprioritize where my energy is. So I'm grateful for it, even though I don't want it. Talk about dichotomy! Yeah, I'm grateful.

And it's uncomfortable. I hate to keep going back to the physical component, but even in a good cycling class, when things are uncomfortable, that's when growth is happening. If you meet the challenge of the uncomfortable, if you step outside the box, if you push yourself a little bit to face it... then you're growing.

Without these uncomfortable moments, I wouldn't see my kids in a different light. I wouldn't shift into a different role as their parent. And nothing should be static...everything should change.

What would Grief say to you?
I think Grief would laugh and say, 'Hang on, we're not done yet!' Grief would say, "As you're now learning, this is not a one-dimensional journey.' Sometimes I'm going to find pockets of grief in moments of joy, as I did with sending my second born off to college. Yes, joy and excitement can coexist with grief and sadness in certain moments. That doesn't make grief not real. It doesn't mean you let the joy and excitement overshadow the grief.

Grief would say 'I'm going to continue to be here in all the moments – in your highs as well as your lows. Keep embracing me for your highest growth.'

Candace Sjogren, Grief through the death of a child

What would you say to Grief?
Thank you, Grief, for coming to visit me. For showing me what I'm capable of, for teaching me the depths of my ability to love, for allowing me to fall so deeply in love to understand the power of humanity and how to appreciate life.

What would Grief say to you?
Dear Mama, you are so powerful because you feel so much and so deeply. And you love so deeply because you allow yourself to go all the way down...to reach...so you can understand. That is your superpower and that's why I'm here for you. This is how you are able to relate so deeply with other humans. And it's a gift that only I could show you. Thank you.

Missy Spears, Grief through divorce

What would you say to Grief?
Will there ever be a time when I don't feel you? I've been through other heartbreaks and breakups, but nothing sits as heavy as the first time I learned that love isn't enough, and it's always hung around like a cloud warning me.

What would Grief say to you?
Suck it up, get off your ass, and do something of value with your life. You owe it.

Candice Terrell, Grief through letting go of people who are still living

What would you say to Grief?
You're allowed to be here. It's okay. I'm not trying to push you away, even though it's hard and sometimes I want it to be done. I know I have to feel it to heal. I know that this is just part of it. So, I think that's what I would tell my grief - you're allowed to be here with me right now, not forever, but at least right now. As long as it takes, it's okay.

What would Grief say to you?
Oh gosh, maybe...I'm proud of you.

I think grief knows that this is one of the hardest things I've ever been through. But it's holding me.... we're in this together. Yeah, it's proud of me...we're proud of us. And it's gonna be okay.

Michael, Grief as a child through his parent's divorce

What would you say to Grief?
Thank you. You've done your job, and you've been here quite a while. I hope you've enjoyed your stay in my mind...I know it's messy up there sometimes.

What would Grief say to you?
I'm not sure what grief would say to me....probably something about how despite everything that's happened, I'm still me. But I still feel like it'd have its own way of saying things that I can't quite fathom.

Maria Lees Dunlap, Grief through divorce

What would you say to Grief?
I think the greatest thing I learned about grief is that grief is the witness of the depth of our love. It is such a gift to be able to love, and if we don't truly love, we really can't experience grief. And as crappy as grief is, and as chaotic as it is, and messy as it can be, and frustrating and isolating and hard – all of these things that we want to put with grief, I guess I think at the end of the day, if this is what I got to experience, because I gave all of my heart to something, then I'll take it. I trust it. I'm grateful to have seen and experienced the resilience in my life, to know that love is worth the grief, because the grief is going to lead me to resilience and I'll be able to do it again.

What would Grief say to you?
Honestly, I think my grief would say to me, I'm really proud of you. I'm really proud of you.

A couple days after reflecting, Maria publicly shared this additional reflection:

Two questions rocked me this week.
My dear friend, Krista Powers, had the wisdom and grace

*to ask me during an interview for her book releasing this fall, **Good Grief**.*
And in all my years of grief work...
I had never asked them, and honestly, have not really considered them either.

What would you say to grief?
Thank you.
You've shaped me.
You catapulted me into purpose, passion, and possibility.
You cracked me open so I could lean into my becoming.
With you, I've learned—
I am capable of hard things.
I am courageous.
I live in resilience.

What would grief say to you?
I am proud of you.
You've taken the sharpness, the sleepless nights, the ache, the confusion—And surrendered to the magic and mystery of beautiful brokenness. What's growing inside you is bright.
Bold.
Unstoppable.
You, my dear, are a warrior.
These questions unraveled me...but they also anchored me.
Grief is not just pain.
It's a portal.
A teacher.
A companion.
A mirror.
So I ask you now:
What would you say to your grief?
And what would grief say to you?

Acknowledgements

To Patrick ~
Good grief, indeed!
My Love, you have been present in the depths of my grief –
never rushing or pushing – yet always reminding me that
there is power in it all. Thank you for bearing witness to my
life, allowing me to do the same for you, and for co-creating
a relationship that ripples love into the world.

To Jessie ~
We have traversed a lot of grief together. Thank you for
inviting me to trust, to learn, and to grow. I am in awe of
your wisdom and heart!

To Brian Shircliff & the VITALITY Cincinnati Community ~
Twice now, you have allowed me to birth something special.
Thank you for being a conduit for dreams and vision to spring
forth – for me and for many.

To those who said *"Yes"* to my request to discuss grief – from
their own personal and professional journeys. **Jackson
Athey, Jessie Cybrowski, Nan Fischer, Patrick
Flerlage, Lacey Fox, Anne Gerber, Kris Girrell,
Forrest Horn, Elizabeth Huffman, Stephen McIntosh,
Tammy Miller-Ploetz, Megan Mitchell, Michele
Mischler, Dianne Powers, Thom Powers, Lindsey
Simons, Candace Sjogren, Missy Spears, Michael,
Candice Terrell, Maria Lees-Dunlap** – you, dear hearts,
cracked my heart open! Your vulnerability and honesty created
compassion and connection within me as I listened to your
story, and I can assure you it will have the same effect on
countless others. Thank you. Namaste.

About the Author

Krista Powers is a powerful catalyst and committed contributor to the communal conversation about grief. As the Executive Director of Giving Voice Foundation, she dedicates her work to building essential connections and providing support for those impacted by dementia. Drawing on three decades of service across healthcare, nonprofit, education, and business sectors, Krista is a dynamic author, speaker, and coach. A two-time cancer-thriver, she passionately shines a light on the inherent power of every human in both professional and personal settings. She is overjoyed to be creating a family with her partner, Patrick, and two creative and kind kids in Covington, Kentucky.

KristaPowers.com

About VITALITY

VITALITY is a circle of friends welcoming all, awakening each other, and reminding each other that we are Whole.

Our affordable self-care programs invite everyone to move, to breathe, to rest, to contemplate, to grow... wherever each person begins their self-care journey, wherever and however they want to become.

It's the power of a circle!

We invite you to explore with us through our

donation-based drop-in classes...
in person & via Zoom

affordable trainings

individual sessions

volunteer opportunities

vitalitycincinnati.org

VITALITY

buzz, bliss + books

publishing books from VITALITY's circle of friends
inspiring love, creativity, + possibility

vitalitybuzz.org